Life as an Intelligence Test
The Predictive Power of IQ

Anthony Walsh
Boise State University

Cognitive Science and Psychology

VERNON PRESS

www.vernonpress.com

In the Americas:	*In the rest of the world:*
Vernon Press	Vernon Press
1000 N West Street, Suite 1200	C/Sancti Espiritu 17,
Wilmington, Delaware, 19801	Malaga, 29006
United States	Spain

Cognitive Science and Psychology

Library of Congress Control Number: 2023940492

ISBN: 978-1-64889-920-1

Also available: 978-1-64889-716-0 [Hardback]; 978-1-64889-739-9 [PDF, E-Book]

Table of Contents

Preface

Human beings have a wide array of characteristics that distinguish them from other species, but their cognitive abilities distinguish them most clearly. Humans do not have great strength, speed, ferocity, or natural weapons to enable them to meet the needs of survival, but their intelligence does a much better job and has enabled them to become masters of the Earth. Intelligence has enabled humans to plumb the mysteries of nature's laws and adapt them to their needs. By the power of the intellect, we have harnessed the laws of nature to the extent that we can traverse continents at a far greater speed than any animal by at least a factor of ten, cross vast oceans (both on them and under them) far faster than any sea creature, and fly further and exponentially faster than any bird. It is also unfortunately true that our understanding of the laws of nature has made us the most dangerous species on Earth; stronger and more ferocious than any other creature, capable of killing millions with the push of a button. The human cognitive abilities of consciousness, language, self-awareness, theory of mind, and abstract symbolic representation seem far in excess of the abilities required to meet nature's twin survival and reproduction imperatives.

Every human being is intelligent, but some are more intelligent than others. We know this by observations of people's behavior and their achieved position in life. We also know it by intelligence quotient (IQ) scores that vary immensely among people. Most of the business of life can be conducted on the basis of habit, with little need for high intelligence, which is largely irrelevant to many day-to-day pursuits. However, people of higher intelligence do much better in life than those of lower intelligence in so many ways, and much of life is an intelligence test. I borrowed the title and the idea for this book from Robert Gordon's (1997) article: "Everyday life as an intelligence test: Effects of intelligence and intelligence."

There are more than a few egalitarian people in academia who balk at the concept of intelligence, particularly its assessment via IQ tests, precisely because it leads to so many life outcomes that separate people and can lead to invidious comparisons. Yet the reliability and validity obtained from these test scores sit head and shoulders above those of any other pencil and paper measures of human traits and characteristics. Others deny that there is a single monolithic intelligence and that there are multiple intelligences that IQ tests do not capture. There are indeed many human talents that we usually don't think of as being intellectual, but if they involve taxing the mind, they engage measurable intelligence.

IQ tests measure different cognitive abilities, but there is a factor common to them all that psychometricians call *Spearman's g*, or simply *g*. What this means is that in tasks that tax the brain, however different they may be from one another, if a person is good at one mental task, he or she is likely to be good at others, although not necessarily to the same degree. Because of the painful issue of race differences in IQ, many have claimed that IQ tests are biased in favor of White middle-class subjects, but IQ predicts many life outcomes equally for all races. Others who acknowledge the racial differences counsel that they should nevertheless be denied lest they be used to give aid racist agendas. I examine the evidence related to these issues and find none that point to bias, although there is evidence that some factors, such as motivation and stereotype threat, can reduce people's IQ scores. However, these factors have no bearing on the issue of test bias.

Chapters three and four examine the biological underpinnings of intelligence. They examine evolutionary scenarios (e.g., Cold Winters Theory) contributing to the evolution of the human brain and the genetics of intelligence (the selection of alleles by new environmental challenges). Both chapters emphasize the role of the environment, first in the development of the brain and then its role in the expression of genetic potential. The purely environmental contributions to intelligence, both in enhancing and reducing it, and the Fynn Effect are addressed in chapter five. Some reasons offered in the literature for the Flynn Effect are explored, as are reasons offered for its cessation and reversal in Western countries.

So many of life's outcomes are predicted by intelligence. The remaining three chapters look at three of the most important to social science. The first is socioeconomic status (SES), which predicts many other things. The second examines various health issues and the third looks at criminal behavior. Above-average IQ successfully predicts higher levels of socioeconomic success, good health, and prosocial behavior. Below-average IQ successfully predicts the opposite. Some scholars reject the notion that IQ predicts any of these phenomena but the evidence that is does too overwhelming to be cavalierly dismissed.

Acknowledgments

I would first like to acknowledge the acquisitions editor Blanca Caro for her faith in this work and production editor Argiris Legatos for his usual great job in moving this book forward into print. I also would like to thank anonymous reviewers for their excellent criticisms and suggestions. The input from these good people has made this book better than it would otherwise have been. Of course, whatever errors that remain are mine alone. Most of all, I thank God for giving me the time, inclination, and insight to be able to complete this work. I also acknowledge the contribution of my dear and most gorgeous wife, Grace (AKA "Grace the Face"). She takes such great care of my needs that I am able to devote far more time to writing than I would otherwise have. She makes my life heaven on earth: thank you, Gracie. Nagyon szeretlek gyönyörű kapálós edényem!

Chapter 1

The Concept and Measurement of Intelligence

What is Meant by Intelligence?

This book looks at the relationship between intelligence and areas of social significance, such as socioeconomic status, health, criminal behavior, and a host of other phenomena that are studied by sociologists, psychologists, and economists. The role of intelligence in everyday life is all too often unappreciated and underestimated. When we hear the word "intelligence," we understand what it means; yet strange as it may seem to the layperson, some folks in academia find intelligence to be an ill-defined and controversial notion. Stuart Ritchie (2015, p. 8) warns us: "Just mention IQ in polite company, and you'll be informed (sometimes rather sternly) that IQ tests don't measure anything real and reflect only how good you are at doing IQ tests ... and that those who are interested in intelligence testing must be elitists, or perhaps something more sinister." It is indeed strange that some people look at what is perhaps the human specie's most defining characteristic this way.

Ritchie is passionate about the role of intelligence in social life, but Henry Schlinger (2003) writes of "the myth of intelligence" and accuses British psychologist and statistician Charles Spearman, one of the pioneers of the scientific study of intelligence, of reifying it: "He took an abstract mathematical correlation and reified it as the general intelligence that someone possesses" (p. 17). He also writes: "We are fooled into believing that the term refers to a tangible entity because other words in our language, such as cat or table, have tangible referents" (p. 24) and that "some psychologists persist in believing in intelligence is that they have a significant personal and professional investment in it" (p. 29). This is a pretty bizarre statement. He is saying that because intelligence is an abstraction and not a tangible material thing, it does not exist, and intelligence researchers can't let it go because they have so much invested in it. For something to be "really real," in his view, it must occupy space and have form. This is an extreme form of philosophical nominalism.

Seventeenth-century French philosopher and mathematician Rene Descartes expressed the whole of reality in terms of abstraction. He began his most famous argument by stating that good philosophy entails doubting everything, even one's existence, so he searched for something that he could not possibly doubt. Descartes noted that we can doubt anything except that we doubt, and doubting is thinking. Thus, the only thing we can be absolutely certain of is that we think, as his famous dictum asserts: "*Cogito ergo sum*" affirms. Doubting one's existence serves as proof of the reality of one's mind, and that proves there is an entity doing the thinking, namely the self. But how do we define a mind except to say that it is the abstract "something" with which we think? This may not be a satisfactory definition since we have defined it only in terms of what it does—moving concepts, problems, perceptions, and so on around in our heads. It is a tautology akin to the standard definition of energy as the "capacity to do work." You can't see, touch, weigh, or smell energy; it is an intangible "something" only indirectly observed as it moves physical things around. Despite its centrality to physics, Nobel laureate Richard Feynman tells us that: "It is important to realize that in physics today, we have no knowledge of what energy is" (in Hecht, 2007, p. 88). It is represented in mathematical terms by which we can make useful predictions and is operationalized and quantified by concepts such as joules, calories, kilowatts, etc., but its essence, what it actually *is*, still eludes physics.

We can think of intelligence similarly as operationalized "mental energy" that moves the concepts of our minds around to find adaptive solutions to the problems of life. Like the physicists' energy, we can quantify mental energy by scores on IQ tests and/or various physiological tests such as reaction time and the brain's glucose consumption, and those scores tell us how much mental work people are capable of. The Latin root word of intelligence is *intelligo* ("to select among"). Intelligence thus implies the ability to select from among a variety of mental elements and to analyze, synthesize, and arrange them in such a way as to provide satisfactory, and sometimes novel, solutions to problems the elements may pose. The speed and efficiency with which this is done differ greatly among people, and that is what psychologists call intelligence. Having said that, we should acknowledge that IQ is not synonymous with intelligence. There is more to intelligence than one's IQ score on a test, although they are the only way we have of consistently operationalizing the concept, and it has great predictive power.

To assess the level of agreement among experts on important elements of intelligence, Snyderman and Rothman (1988) surveyed 1,020 PhDs in developmental psychology and behavioral genetics. Responses were placed into three categories: (1) those for which there was virtual unanimity: "abstract thinking or reasoning," checked by 99.3%, "problem-solving ability," 97.7%; and "capacity to acquire knowledge," by 96%; (2) those checked by the majority; "memory," 80.5%, "adaptation to one's environment," 77.2%, and "mental speed," 71.7%; (3) those rarely checked included "achievement motivation,"

18.9% and "goal-directedness," 24%. These elements conform to David Wechsler's (who devised many of today's intelligence tests) definition of intelligence: "The aggregate or global capacity of the individual to act purposefully, to think rationally, and to deal effectively with his environment. It is aggregate or global because it is composed of elements or abilities (features) which, although not entirely independent, are qualitatively differentiable" (in Matarazzo, 1976, p. 79).

The terms *aggregate* and *global* recognize that different mental tests measure different cognitive abilities but also that there is a factor common to them all. Psychometricians call this common factor *Spearman's g*, or simply *g*, which is a statistical measure derived from factor analyses of a variety of separate tests represented by the first unrotated principal component. Spearman's *g* ("*g*" for "general" intelligence) is the only factor common to all measures of intelligence. What this means is that in any tasks that tax the brain, however different they may be from one another, if a person is good at one mental task, he or she is likely to be good at others, although not necessarily to the same degree (the correlation between a specific test and the general factor across a number of mental tests are mostly in the range of 0.50 to 0.90) (Deary, Spinath, & Bates, 2006). Thus, there is no measure of cognitive ability that is independent of *g*, and psychometricians agree that *g* conforms to what both they and laypersons mean by intelligence (Buschkuehl, & Jaeggi, 2010).

Despite its naysayers, intelligence is immensely important. Humans have many tools in their tool boxes to navigate their lives that are context-specific, but intelligence is a more general tool that is useful in almost all contexts. It is perhaps the "master" attribute that differentiates humans from other animals. Non-human animals are well-adapted to their environments in which they instinctively respond to stimuli, but they cannot create alternate environments. Humans are also well-adapted to their environments, but they can adapt to any environment and even create new ones. Intelligence has always been of prime importance to our species, but it is particularly important in increasingly more complex societies in which strong backs and broad shoulders alone no longer suffice to move one ahead in the world unless one is a professional athlete. As Linda Gottfredson noted: "Intelligence has a profound effect on the structure of society, not necessarily because it is the most highly valued of individual differences—although conceivably it is—but rather because it may have the widest and most stable distribution among all the traits that are valuable in industrialized nations" (1986, p. 406).

IQ Subscales

Intelligence is measured by IQ tests which are composed of verbal IQ (VIQ) and Performance IQ (PIQ). These two subscales are combined to give a measure of an individual's full-scale IQ (FSIQ). There is a variety of IQ tests for people of all ages with different levels of difficulty. The higher a test's g-load, and the more it is g-loaded, the more it depends on the common g factor rather than on a specific content domain, and the greater its complexity and the more g-loaded a test, the higher its heritability (Lubinski, 2004). The Raven Standard Progressive Matrices test is the most widely used of all tests of intelligence because it relies minimally on cultural learning, is recognized as the best measure of general intelligence, and has the highest loading on the g factor of all IQ tests (Arce-Ferrer, & Martinez Guzman, 2009). It has reported split-half, test-retest, and internal consistency reliabilities of between 0.80 and 0.90 (Arce-Ferrer, & Martinez Guzman, 2009; Prokosch, Yeo, & Miller, 2005). This level of reliability sits head and shoulders above the reliability of all other pencil and paper psychological measures. The validity, especially criterion-related validity—measures of the degree to which a scale measures what it is supposed to measure and predicts what it ought to predict—of intelligence tests is something we will be looking at frequently.

Below is a normalized distribution of full-scale IQ scores. The further to the right of this figure individuals are, the more they will be able to achieve intellectually. On the other hand, most criminal offenders fall in the 85-to-100 range (Ellis & Walsh, 2003; Wilson & Herrnstein, 1985).

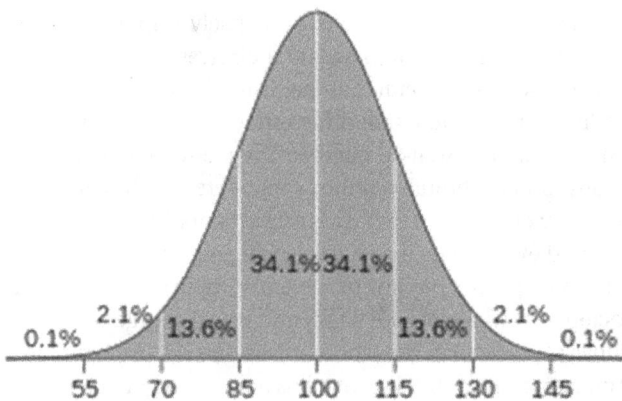

Figure 1.1. Normalized distribution of IQ with mean of 100 and standard deviation of 15. Source: Wikimedia Commons, the free media repository.

Typical VIQ subscale measures are:

Information: common knowledge of everyday life.
Comprehension: the ability to draw logical conclusions about situations in everyday life.

Arithmetic: logical thinking and simple calculation with numbers.
Vocabulary: knowledge of the meaning of words.
Similarities: the ability to form and logically compare verbal concepts.
Digit Span: attention to sequential numbers both forward and backward.

Typical PIQ subscale measures are:

Object Assembly: the ability to visualize and form wholeness from parts of an object.
Block Design: logical visuospatial organization and problem-solving.
Mazes: visuomotor surveying mazes and route planning.
Picture Arrangement: organizing pictures in a logical manner.
Coding: working speed while coding symbols.
Picture Completion: ability to pay close attention to find missing details in pictures.

Below are examples of items on a typical IQ test taken by schoolchildren. Note that they require no more than the ability to read the English language, the kind of elementary mathematics acquired by at least the fourth grade, and the exercise of simple logic.

A sea captain is caught in a bad storm one mile from the coast. If he steers toward the land, he will be shipwrecked; if he steers toward the open sea, he will also be shipwrecked. He must steer one way or the other, so which of the below is correct:

1. He should steer toward the open sea.
2. He should steer toward the land.
3. The coast is always dangerous for ships.
4. The ship will be wrecked.
5. This will be his last voyage.
   Answer, 4.

What number comes next in this sequence?

3, 7, 16, 35, ?

Answer, 74; 3 is doubled plus 1; 7 is doubled plus 2, and 16 is doubled plus 3, etc.

What number is missing from this sequence?

4, 9, 25, ? 49, 64

   Answer, 36. Each number is a square.

Find the word below that is closest in meaning to "angry."

1. Emotional
2. Insulted
3. Annoyed
4. Passionate
5. Depressed
   Answer, 3.

A big car is to driving as a big book is to

1. Page numbers
2. Weight
3. Reading
4. Enjoyment
5. Difficulty
   Answer, 3.

It should be noted that there are no significant sex differences today in verbal and performance IQ scores despite robust sex differences on other measures of verbal (females better) and visuospatial abilities (males better). This non-significance is purposely designed into modern IQ tests. The initial Wechsler IQ tests did show highly significant sex differences between the sub-scales in the expected directions (females significantly greater VIQ; males significantly greater PIQ), but Wechsler wanted a sex-neutral measure of intelligence, not a measure of verbal and visual-spatial abilities per se. He achieved this by pruning the items on each subscale most responsible for the sex difference; thus, today's items index verbal or performance skills less strongly than did the original items (Wells, 1980).

Crystallized and Fluid Intelligence

General intelligence consists of two forms of intelligence: crystallized and fluid. These two forms of intelligence are characterized by somewhat different neurocognitive architectures (Simpson-Kent et al., 2020). Crystallized intelligence is heavily dependent on acquired knowledge and refers to the ability to use skills and knowledge acquired via prior learning, while fluid intelligence reflects the ability to analyze problems in novel ways and relies minimally upon prior learning. Fluid intelligence is more strongly related to mathematical and more complex logical skills than to reading and foundation skills. Fluid intelligence is: "the ability to cope with new situations for which previously acquired knowledge is only minimally useful" (Buschkuehl & Jaeggi, 2010, p. 266). Fluid intelligence is, therefore, an "on-the-spot" cognitive *process*, and crystallized intelligence is the stored *product* of learning. You can increase your crystallized intelligence by learning different things, but whether fluid intelligence in healthy individuals can be increased remains a matter of contention (Hayes, Petrov, & Sederberg, 2015). We can certainly improve our fluid intelligence scores on IQ tests with practice, but whether this translates into real-world situations is conjectural. Most items on modern tests rely heavily on items that tap into fluid intelligence to minimize the effects of acquired knowledge and thus evidence bias because of different levels of educational attainment. Because IQ tests are given to people of all ages, all test item difficulties are adjusted to their age.

People with high fluid intelligence have an easier time acquiring knowledge than those with lower fluid intelligence, so fluid and crystallized intelligence are strongly related. Both forms of intelligence are used in many different circumstances. For example, when taking an exam in mathematics, people rely on fluid intelligence to construct a strategy to come up with the right answer. Crystallized intelligence is also needed to recall the correct mathematical concepts (such as the foil method in algebra or the Pythagorean theorem in geometry) before fluid intelligence is engaged to arrive at the correct answers. With practice, over time, the mathematical concepts will be engaged largely automatically and no longer require the use of fluid intelligence because they have become part of one's store of crystallized knowledge. Thus, fluid and crystallized intelligence work together synergistically. Lechner, Miyamoto, and Knopf (2019, p. 10) ask if students should be smart (fluid intelligence), curious (open and interested in specific subjects), or both. They answer their question by informing us that:

> gf [g fluid] and interest interacted in a synergistic fashion in shaping (gains in) gc [g crystallized]. This held true for both of the domains that we investigated, reading and math. A synergistic interaction implies that high levels of one trait cannot compensate for low levels of the other—being "smart" (i.e., having high gf) and "curious" (i.e., being interested in a subject) are both essential traits for knowledge acquisition, and students with high levels of both traits experience the strongest gains in gc.

The crystallized-fluid distinction tells us why intelligence is not learned in the traditional sense of education. Intelligence is not how much you know but your capacity to know. If intelligence (as opposed to knowledge) was acquired through education, it would increase dramatically across the life course as knowledge increases, but it does not. IQ scores are remarkably stable across the life course, with test-retest correlations as high as 0.94 over a 10-year span (Deary et al., 2000), and remain stable even as a person acquires vast storehouses of knowledge from childhood to old age. A 60-year-old college professor may have acquired the knowledge to pontificate on subjects that would have mystified him or her at age 15, but despite huge increases in knowledge, his or her IQ would differ minimally at age 60 from what it was at 15, and his or her fluid intelligence may have even declined a little. It is fairly well agreed upon that fluid intelligence increases into early adulthood before steadily decreasing as we age (Deary, Johnson, & Houlihan, 2009; Simpson-Kent et al., 2020). This does not necessarily mean that intelligence is impervious to change; stability does not mean fixity.

High IQ Does Not Necessarily Imply Wisdom

Amassing large amounts of intellectual knowledge and a high IQ does not necessarily make one wise. I venture to predict that if we had a measure of wisdom akin to an IQ test with the same reliability and validity, that wisdom and IQ would positively correlate only moderately. Many of us have much knowledge, but few of us have much wisdom. Wisdom is a mysterious "something" that implies the ability of discernment, the right judgment, and the ability to use one's knowledge to give one's life perspective and meaning. It is also the quality of humbly admitting that we can be very wrong in both the factual truth of our knowledge and/or our interpretations of it. According to Dutton and van der Linden (2015), the average IQ of social science Ph.Ds is 123, which is impressive, but as we have to admit, there are a lot of what physician and evolutionary psychologist Bruce Charlton calls "clever sillies" among us. Clever sillies are intellectuals that embrace ideas "about social phenomena that are not just randomly inaccurate (due to inappropriately misapplying abstract analysis) by are *systematically* wrong" (2009, p. 869). Charlton is referring to ideas such as postmodernism and utopianism that spring from what he calls "IQ-advertising" ("I must be smart; my work puzzles so many people"). He maintains that many academics in the social sciences overthink social phenomena to the point of utter confusion in matters where common sense, built into us over eons of evolutionary time, would better suffice. A clever, silly state:

is a somewhat tragic state; because it entails being cognitively trapped by compulsive abstraction; unable to engage directly and spontaneously with what most humans have traditionally regarded as psycho-social reality; disbarred from the common experience of humankind and instead cut-adrift on the surface of a glittering but shallow ocean of novelties: none of which can ever truly convince or satisfy. It is to be alienated from the world; and to find no stable meaning of life that is solidly underpinned by emotional conviction" (2009, p. 869).

Charlton is not dismissive of abstract thinking in the hard sciences, which explore evolutionarily novel and counter-intuitive phenomena. Struggling with theoretical physics, for instance, it is sometimes necessary to take ideas beyond the orthodoxy of the moment by overriding the common sense "Darwinian brain." However, abstract analysis is not usually useful for dealing with social issues for which humans have evolved a much-underappreciated common sense. Dutton and van der Linden opine: "An idea is 'clever silly' if it is founded on the acceptance of a dogma which either has strong empirical evidence against it or otherwise by its very nature cannot be disproven but which, nevertheless, allows the advocate to advertise their intelligence by virtue of the idea being highly complex and/or original" (2015, p. 58).

Physicist Alan Sokal provides a telling example of the susceptibility to folly among presumably high IQ Ph.Ds. He planted a booby trap that his targets stepped into in the form of an article titled *Transgressing the Boundaries: Toward a transformative hermeneutics of quantum gravity* (1996). Sokal's parody was published in the Marxist cultural studies journal *Social Text*. The article purported to demonstrate that quantum gravity was just a social construct with political implications and is "clearly...an archetypal postmodernist science" (Sokal & Bickmont, 1998, p. 234). His satire was accepted as a serious contribution, although it was copiously salted with pure nonsense. It is so impeccably adorned with impenetrable postmodernist prose that Sokal was able to easily sneak it into the camp as a Trojan horse, where it was received as a flattering gift from a physicist who apparently endorsed the journal's view of the world. Sokal later revealed his hoax in the magazine *Lingua Franca*, where he described it as "a mélange of truths, half-truths, quarter truths, falsehoods, non-sequiturs, and syntactically correct sentences *that have no meaning at all*" (Sokal & Bickmont, 1998, pp. 208-209; emphasis added).

Upon hearing the article was a hoax, the aggrieved editors of *Social Text* and those who drink at its trough, unable to distinguish between the meaningful and the meaningless, whined like losers in the locker room about their opponent's perfidious tactics. *Social Text* editors said they believed his article to be: "the earnest attempt of a professional scientist to seek some kind of affirmation from postmodern philosophy for developments in his field. All of us were distressed at the deceptive means by which Sokal chose to make his point. This breach of ethics is a serious matter in any scholarly community, and has damaging consequences when it occurs in science publishing" (Robbins & Ross, 1996). The idea that postmodern philosophy could lead to "developments" in physics or that the *Social Text* is "science publishing" adds further knee-slapping levity to the hoax. This reminds me of the old adage: "It is better to remain silent at the risk of being thought a fool than to talk and remove all doubt of it."

Chapter 2

Are IQ Tests Culturally Biased?

The Painful Issue of Racial Differences

Unlike issues in the physical and natural sciences, the social sciences sometimes deal with topics that may be painful to some and may lead to invidious comparisons. The quintessential example of this is racial differences in IQ. Howard Gardner, for instance, writes: "I myself do not condone investigations of racial differences in intelligence, because I think that the results of these studies are likely to be incendiary" (Gardner, 2001, p. 8). Because of this, many social scientists refuse to entertain them, and others may engage in ad hominem attacks on those that do. Intelligence researchers are met with charges of racism, and once the label is applied, it sticks like tar and ruins careers. Researcher scientists such as Arthur Jensen, Michael Levin, and John Philippe Rushton have been mercilessly pilloried for their work, and James Watson was relegated from an eminent Nobel Prize winner to a pariah because of his statements about race and IQ (Ceci & Williams, 2009). What a dark hole of ignorance we would be in had the scientific curmudgeons of the past, such as Galileo and Darwin, been similarly silenced.

Steven Rose (2009, p. 788) is one who dismisses research on race and IQ, saying that racial differences in IQ should not be studied because it is ideology "masquerading as science." Despite Rose's undoubted noble intentions, calling the work of other ideology rather than science is bad form, for such an attitude extinguishes:

> discussion by making moral attributions about their presumed character flaws rather than debating facts. Virtually no other scientific hypothesis is summarily dismissed as race differences in IQ are. Character attacks "lead to a one-party science that squelches divergent views. ... When dissenters' positions are prevented exposure in high-impact journals and excluded from conferences, the dominant side goes unchallenged, and eventually its rationale is forgotten, forestalling the evolution of crucial ideas" (Ceci & Williams, 2009, p. 789).

Searching for "small t" truth and exposing falsehood has always been the most fundamental commitment of science—its categorical imperative—and should always remain so.

The dismissal of race and IQ research reaches its apogee when genes are claimed to be part of the cause of racial differences. Harvard geneticist David Reich acknowledges that findings of a genetic basis for intelligence can be used by racist groups but that to stifle research because of such dangers is counterproductive for several reasons:

> I have deep sympathy for the concern that genetic discoveries about differences among populations may be misused to justify racism. But it is precisely because of this sympathy that I am worried that people who deny the possibility of substantial biological differences among populations across a range of traits are digging themselves into an indefensible position, one that will not survive the onslaught of science. In the last couple of decades, most population geneticists have sought to avoid contradicting the orthodoxy. When asked about the possibility of biological differences among human populations, we have tended to obfuscate, making mathematical statements in the spirit of Richard Lewontin about the average difference between individuals from within any one population being around six times greater than the average difference between populations . . .. But this carefully worded formulation is deliberately masking the possibility of substantial average differences in biological traits across populations. (Reich, 2018, p. 254).

Reich's reference to Richard Lewontin refers to Lewontin's claim that individuals from within one population differ genetically about six times more than the average difference between populations which was meant to deny the existence of human races rather a statement about intelligence, but his statement is probably the most quoted statement in social science relevant to race. This requiem for race was penned by Lewontin in 1972. Although his claim was challenged by other geneticists at the time, these challenges were ignored until 2003 when A.W.F. Edwards, who developed many of the techniques on which population genetics depends, did so. Edwards argued that Lewontin performed his analysis to attack racial classification which he detested for social and not scientific reasons, and called his work a "superficial analysis" (2003, p. 799). He showed that Lewontin was correct when examining differences in a single genetic locus between individuals, but the probability of racial misclassification rapidly approaches zero when as few as 20 loci are examined. Ian Hacking notes that: "Edwards' analysis is, for anyone with a modest statistical training, rather direct and self-evident," and states that Edwards' work "is now widely judged as correct" (2006, p. 85-86).

Following the media brouhaha following the publication of *The Bell Curve* by Herrnstein and Murry in 1994, the American Psychological Association (APA) commissioned a task force of eleven leading experts on intelligence to evaluate claims made in the book, particularly the consistent black/white difference in average IQ. The Black/White difference is not in itself controversial; what is controversial is why it exists. The task force wrote: "the Black mean is typically about one standard deviation (about 15 points) below that of Whites" (Neisser et al. 1996, p. 93). There is no shortage of explanations for why this gap exists, but I see no merit in denying the existence of this gap when one is well aware that it exists, as Nathaniel Glazer did. Referring to Herrnstein and Murry's contention that society is living a lie with regard to IQ, he responded: "I ask myself whether the untruth is not better for American society than the truth" (1994, p. 16). Galileo Galilei, the father of modern science, would have been appalled at this regardless of motive. He once said that: "Who does not know the truth, is simply a fool...Yet who knows the truth and calls it a lie, is a criminal" (in Pirnahad, 2007, p. 84). Linda Gottfredson notes that this untruth can only deepen racial animosities, "Because the untruth insists that differences cannot be natural, they must be artificial, manmade, manufactured. Someone must be at fault. Someone must be refusing to do the right thing" (2005, p. 318).

The Issue of Test Bias

As valuable as intelligence doubtless is to understanding many facets of human life, we must not confuse it with moral worth—there are many saints among the dull and many sinners among the bright. As Herrnstein and Murray (1994, p. 21) point out: "one of the problems of writing about intelligence is how to remind readers often enough how little IQ scores tell you about whether the human being next to you is someone you will admire or cherish." Because the racial gap cannot be denied, the focus of the assault on IQ has been tested biased. IQ tests (the predictor variable) would be biased if the regression slopes for individuals of identical IQs from different racial groups were significantly different on some criterion variable, but they are not. IQ tests are not biased simply because different groups have different mean scores. The APA task force (1996) maintained that IQ scores predict a wide range of outcomes equally well across all human categories in the United States and are therefore not biased. The tests would be biased if they accurately predicted performance (school grades; occupational success, etc.) for middle-class Whites but not for other races or classes, or if different races and social classes were stumped by different test items. But this is not the case; the rank ordering of relative difficulty of test items is almost identical for Blacks and Whites and across social classes (Snyderman & Rothman, 1988). In other words, the items that Blacks find most difficult are also the most difficult items for Whites.

Despite all the evidence against them, like a trial lawyer with a poor case, IQ naysayers shout louder and louder as their case gets weaker and weaker. The only evidence they bring to the bench is that different groups consistently show different average scores, and since all groups should be equal in their cognitive ability, the tests are *ipso-facto*-biased. This is an example of the moralist fallacy rife in some areas; there *should* be no group difference in IQ; therefore, there *is* not, and if there is, it is the fault of the test. The reliability and validity of IQ tests rise to levels above all other measures of human traits and abilities. We must live with these findings and incorporate them into our thinking rather than condemn them or deny their existence. Apparently, taller men entering the business world are more likely to be hired than shorter men, to receive higher starting salaries, and to enjoy better promotion prospects (Ellis, 1995). This strikes me as unfair, but it does not lead me to question the reliability and validity of yardsticks. Some people are tall, some are short, and some people score higher on IQ tests than others. To blame the instruments that measure these differences for the differences is like burning the yardstick because it puts you on the wrong side of average height. IQ scores, like height and weight, are the result of environmental circumstances interacting with a genetic endowment; the instruments that reveal the unwelcome truths are entirely innocent.

There are doubtless many reasons that some children manifest low scores on IQ tests that have nothing to do with their latent intelligence. We will address some of these reasons later, but for now, we examine the motivation of test takers. Motivation to do well influences any kind of performance, but recall that motivation was not considered a particularly important element of IQ by Snyderman and Rothman's (1988) sample of experts. It is undeniable that IQ scores do not perfectly capture people's latent intelligence; they can only come close when a test taker is highly motivated to do well. Such people are those who are competitive, take pride in their efforts, and anxious to comply with teachers, and have parents (and others) they wish to please. This is intrinsic motivation. Duckworth et al. (2011) looked and a number of *extrinsic* motivational studies and found that providing material incentives (money, tokens, candy) to low- IQ children improved their IQ scores by an average of almost one standard deviation (just over one-fourth of an SD for high-IQ children). Thus, if some individuals perceive the test to have low-outcome stakes for them, they are less than optimally motivated.

It should be noted, however, that this study has not been replicated well. Bates and Gignac (2022, np) address this in three randomized control tests and conclude:

> In three randomized control tests of the effects of monetary incentive on test scores (total $N = 1201$), incentive effects were statistically non-significant in each study, showed no dose dependency, and jointly indicated an effect one quarter the size previously estimated ($d = 0.166$). These results suggest that, in neurotypical adults, individual differences

in test motivation have, on average, a negligible influence on intelligence test performance. ($\approx$ 2.5 IQ points). The association between test motivation and test performance likely partly reflects differences in ability, and subjective effort partly reflects outcome expectations.

It is difficult to gauge motivation in non-experimental settings in which extrinsic incentives are not provided, but its impact on IQ testing is often assessed by results from the digit-span subtests of IQ scales. The digit-span tests consist of a series of numbers given orally by the examiner, which subjects are to repeat both forward and backward. Backward repetition is more mentally taxing, and the Black/White difference is close to twice as great for backward than for forward repetition (Jensen, & Figueroa, 1975). Such findings represent something of a puzzle, for if we maintain that differential motivation explains the difference in Black/White scores, we will have to explain how Black subjects become more unmotivated when repeating digits backward. However, this was the only study I could find specifically testing this digit span hypothesis, so it should be treated with caution.

One of the efforts to prove that IQ tests are biased has a kind of logic to it if one accepts the premise that they are culturally biased. If IQ tests merely measure the content of white middle-class culture, as many maintain, it is no wonder that we find the persistent 15-point gap between the average IQ scores of Blacks and Whites. Sociologist Adrian Dove designed a counter "IQ" test he called the Dove Counterbalance General Intelligence Test (AKA the "Chitling Test") designed to be culturally biased in favor of Blacks. An example of an item on the test is: A "handkerchief head" is: (a) a cool cat, (b) a porter, (c) an Uncle Tom, (d) a hoddi, (e) a preacher (the correct answer is c, an Uncle Tom) (in Laundra & Sutton, 2008). African Americans score much higher than whites on this test, thus providing support for critics' arguments that standard IQ tests measure nothing but the cultural content of white middle-class society in the same way that the Chitling test measures the content of the Black culture.

However, there is not a shred of evidence showing that they successfully predict performance on any important criterion, such as achieving occupational success, criminality, or health outcomes. The Chitling test merely measures knowledge of a particular subculture. Unlike standard IQ tests, they do not measure the ability to reason, evaluate, synthesize, or any of the other cognitive abilities that are needed for success in the larger culture. IQ tests are only "cultural" in the sense that one must be able to read the language in which they are written and know simple arithmetic rules learned by the fourth grade to take most IQ tests. But some continue to maintain that the Chitling test proves that standard IQ tests are biased in favor of Whites. Michael Petty (2010, np) is one scholar that does, and provides us with the test and asks: "Could you answer any of these questions? Blacks in the ghetto could. The main lesson to be learned from the Chitling Test is that all IQ tests are culturally biased."

If Petty believes that IQ tests merely measure the content of White middle-class culture in the same way that the Chitling test measures knowledge of African-American culture, he will have to explain why East Asians, using translations of American IQ tests, typically have an average IQ of 107 (Rushton, 1990) and why mainland Chinese peasants, also using translations of American tests, have an average of 101 (Seligman, 1992). Rindermann, Becker, and Coyle (2016) present a survey of the average IQ of East Asians (Chinese, Japanese, and South Koreans) and find the in excess of all other racial groups. If IQ tests merely measured the content of American White middle-class cultural knowledge, East Asians would score close to zero on both the Chitling test (which they doubtless would) and on standard American IQ tests (which they do not) because neither test is a product of their cultures.

Addressing the Problem Race Differences

The success or failure of any endeavor depends on whether we are guided by truth or falsehood. We cannot properly address a problem if we refuse to admit that it exists. Nathan Cofnas (2020, p. 135) quotes Janet Kourany (2016, pp. 783-784) about what could be done:

> Finding out that blacks have lower IQ scores than whites . . . could be the beginning of educational and training programs to work with the strengths and work on the weaknesses of every group to help make them the very best they can be, and even to use the special talents of each group to help the others. Finding these things out could be the beginning of innovative programs that support rather than undermine the right to equality. That this does not happen, or seldom happens, is a function of the . . . racism of society.

Cofnas concurs with Kourany that such programs ought to exist, but disputes her reasons for why they do not:

> But the reason that these programs, which Kourany rightly says ought to exist, have never been created is not because of racism but because of the taboo on talking about genetic differences among policy makers. No mainstream politician can acknowledge that there are differences that might call for the creation of a program to "work with the strengths and work on the weaknesses of every [ethnic] group to help make them

the very best they can be." It is hereditarians who have advocated these programs and environmentalists who have resisted them (2020, p. 135).

Both Cofnas and Kourany were wrong in asserting that such programs don't exist, although the reason given for them is segregation, not racial differences in IQ. In 1983, Federal district court judge Russell Clarke ruled that the Kansas City, Missouri, Municipal School District had been operating a de facto segregated school system (mainly as a result of "White flight" to the suburbs) and ordered it to remedy the situation as required by federal law. The remedy involved the building of "magnet schools" that would attract White suburban students back to the inner city. The facilities in these magnet schools were described by Justice Anthony Kennedy in his dissent in the case *(Missouri v. Jenkins,* 1990):

> Every school would have a 2,000 square-foot planetarium; greenhouses and vivariums; a 25-acre farm with an air-conditioned meeting room for 104 people; a model United Nations wired for language translation; broadcast capable radio and television studios with an editing and animation lab; a temperature controlled art gallery; movie editing and screening rooms; a 3,500 square-foot dust-free diesel mechanics room; 1,875-square foot elementary school animal rooms for use in a zoo project; swimming pools; and numerous other facilities.

The Kansas City Municipal School District responded to Clarke's ruling by saying that it did not have the funds (an initial total exceeding $200 million, or $596 million in 2022 dollars) to implement the scheme. Clarke ruled that it must find the money and ordered the school district's property tax levy raised from $2.05 to $4.00 per $100 of assessed property value and then later to $4.96 (Gewertz, 2000). Thus, homeowners in the school district saw their property taxes double, with a further 24% added later, and all by judicial fiat—not even George III was that bold! Taking their case to the US Supreme Court, attorneys for the state of Missouri argued that doubling of taxes by order of an unelected, life-tenured federal judge (more correctly, Clarke had ordered county commissioners to do so under pain of contempt of court).

The Supreme Court was not impressed by Missouri's arguments. Authoring the Court's opinion, Justice Byron White reiterated that the Kansas City Municipal School District was segregated, that *Brown v. Board of Education* required desegregation, and that the *Brown* decision placed the onus on local authorities to solve the problem of segregation. Since the local authorities had not done so, it was incumbent on the judiciary to implement the requirement of *Brown* to compel the school district to levy taxes adequate for compliance. That the taxation remedy impacted homeowners presented no problem to the

Court because the ruling "places the responsibility for solutions to the problems of segregation upon those who have themselves created the problems," wrote Justice White. By fleeing to the suburbs, White homeowners were deemed to be responsible for segregation and thus financially responsible for the solution. By mid-1993, the price tag for these schools had exceeded the normal school budget by $1.3 *billion* (2.7 billion in 2022 dollars), and at one point, 44% of the K-12 education budget was being spent on the 9% of students enrolled in the Kansas City and St. Louis magnet schools (Ciotti, 1998). Despite such funding, magnet school students were consistently outscored on all indices of academic achievement by pupils in Missouri's underfunded nonmagnet schools, and many magnet schools even lost their state accreditation (Gewertz, 2000).

A second trip to the Supreme Court *(Missouri v. Jenkins II,* 1995)—based on Missouri's reluctance to provide large, across-the-board salary increases to magnet school teachers given the continued failures of their students and again arguing that underachievement was not attributable to segregation—found a more sympathetic ear. In this decision, the Court reasoned that school segregation was no longer *de jure,* as it had been at the time of *Brown,* but was now the result of *de facto* social forces. The Court also reasoned that the state had done everything practicable to remedy the segregation problem and expressed its wish to see control of the schools back in the hands of local authorities.

Self-Esteem and Stereotype Threat

Kourany (2016, p. 787) suggests that self-esteem among African Americans has been adversely affected by "direct or indirect exposure to the research or aspects of the [IQ] research." Self-esteem is a subjective sense of personal value and describes one's level of confidence in one's abilities to accomplish what one sets out to do. It is thus a very valuable psychological asset. If self-esteem was predicated on "direct or indirect exposure" to IQ research, we should see that Asians have the highest levels of self-esteem, Whites next, followed by Blacks, but it has been repeatedly shown that the pattern is Black >White>Asian; the exact opposite. Meta-analyses have shown that the self-esteem score of Blacks exceeds that of Whites by an average of about 0.15 standard deviation units (Sprecher, Brooks, & Avogo, 2013). Thus, African American self-esteem cannot be invoked as an explanation for their IQ scores.

Negative stereotypes may not adversely affect Black self-esteem, but they appear to have an effect on IQ scores via stereotype threat. "Stereotype threat theory suggests that members of a stigmatized social group are most likely to be threatened by a situational stereotype threat cue when a test is challenging. Because the cognitive demands of a difficult test will increase individuals' mental workload, interference from a stereotype will be cognitively more problematic [physiological stress undermines working memory] when a test is challenging than when a test does not require as much from the test takers' resources" (Nguyen & Ryan, 2008, p. 1316). In other words, simply taking a test given by a White instructor along with mostly White students may trigger stereotype threat due to Black test-takers becoming fearful of confirming the stereotype with poor performance.

In the inaugural study of stereotype threat, Steele & Aronson (1995) reduced threat by telling students they would be solving puzzles rather than taking a test of intellectual ability. They found that controlling for SAT scores, Black participants scored equally with Whites. Of course, controlling for SAT scores is tantamount to using a measure of one cognitive ability to assess the effects of another measure of cognitive ability, which will inevitably reduce the predictive power of IQ. White scores did not vary regardless of being told they told they were taking a test solving puzzles or a test of intellectual ability. Perhaps the lesson to be learned here is simply word substitution; just tell everyone taking an IQ test they are taking a puzzle-solving test, which they, in essence, are. Spencer, Logel, & Davies' (2016) review of the literature showed effect sizes from meta-analyses of stereotype threat ranging from d = 0.46 to d = 0.52. Converting these effect sizes to Pearson correlation coefficients, they range from 0.218 to 0.235; small but statistically significant. Stereotype threat studies, like motivation studies, do not replicate well. Zigerell's (2017) reanalysis of data from the Nguyen and Ryan (2008) stereotype threat date showed effect sizes near zero for the most precise and only small effect sizes for less precise studies when adjusted for publication bias.

Of course, neither the IQ/self-esteem relationship nor the stereotype threat data undermine the reliability or validity of IQ tests any more than does the motivation of test takers. The former simply shows that self-esteem seems to be negatively related (but not causally so) to IQ, and the latter that taking an IQ test under certain conditions adversely affects Black scores. We will be addressing many other factors that depress to IQ scores of disadvantaged groups later. But why mention race at all; why not just ignore it? Gray and Thompson (2004, p. 497) provide one answer: "Given the history of misuse of intelligence research, a statement about biology and intelligence that ignores the question of race can be mistaken as being complicit with a racist agenda. To a non-specialist, the field of intelligence research has become stereotyped as elitist and socially divisive. We disavow — and hope to weaken — these unfortunate and unnecessary associations." It may be divisive, as viewed by both racists and strict egalitarians, but given the increasing complexity of modern societies, the increasing importance of intelligence cannot be denied or ignored.

Chapter 3

The Evolution and Neurobiology of Intelligence

How did Humans Become so Smart?

How did *homo sapiens* become so gifted with intelligence that they gained dominion over the earth? As with all morphological, personality, and behavioral traits, human intelligence evolved from earlier primate intelligence in response to selective pressures generated in ancestral environments. Mother nature has just one "goal;" the continuation of life, and provides all creatures with the tools to make sure that they do what they must to realize that goal. All living things are adapted to their environments, but evolutionarily novel and problematic conditions that were serious enough to have adversely affected survival and reproduction would generate pressure to select genetic mutations that enabled its carriers to solve those problems. For hominins, the most precious tool is the ability to think and reason rationally about the challenges they encounter. As long as the environment stayed stable (i.e., non-problematic in terms of major reoccurring challenges), there would be no such selection pressures, and the gene pool would be in stasis. Gabora and Russon (2011, p. 338) note that after millions of years of hominin evolution, there has been an explosion of innovations requiring ever greater intelligence. The beginning of agriculture and the invention of the wheel only occurred 10,000 to 12,000 years ago (only "yesterday" from an evolutionary perspective), and:

> Written languages developed around 5,000–6,000 years ago, and approximately 4,000 years ago astronomy and mathematics appear on the scene. We see the expression of philosophical ideas around 2,500 years ago, invention of the printing press 1,000 years ago, and the modern scientific method about 500 years ago. The past 100 years have yielded a technological explosion that has completely altered the daily routines of humans. …the consequences of which remain to be seen.

Dealing with all these innovations can be intellectually challenging for older generations, but more easily grasped by the more cognitively gifted among them (many of us remember the problems, the older generation had when personal computers and iPhones first came on the scene). Intelligence is housed in the human brain, the magnum opus of millions of years of evolution. This walnut-shaped, grapefruit-sized, three-pound mass of tofu-like tissue is the most complicated entity in the universe. Nobel laureate Roger Sperry rhapsodized in awe of its complexity and mystery when he wrote: "In the human head there are forces within forces within forces, as in no other cubic half-foot of the universe we know" (in Fincher, 1982, p. 23). The brain constitutes only 2% of body mass, about 50 to 60% of all genes are involved in its development, and it consumes a voracious 20% of the body's energy resources (Mitchell, 2007). Within its buzzing chemical soup and electric sparks lie our thoughts, memories, emotions, and intelligence. Its electrochemical circuitry captures our genetic dispositions and environmental experiences and blends them into an efficient adaptive machine.

The brain is an organ of adaptation supremely calibrated to its environment. Gene-culture co-evolution creates a vast number of opportunities for genetic changes, and the more culture changes, the greater the genomic changes. Genetic mutations—positive, negative, or neutral—will naturally arise more frequently in large mating populations than in smaller ones; this is a mathematical truism. The combination of social, cultural, and ecological pressures, such as moving from tree-based to savanna life and becoming more carnivorous, led to the enlargement of hominid brains, which led to greater intelligence. A larger brain provides more room for more experiences to be encoded and for more associations to be made between and among them (Kanazawa, 2012).

A number of studies of hominin crania dating back to 1.9 million years have shown that cranial capacity increases most rapidly in areas of the globe with greater population density and where food procurement was most problematic; that is, in the colder areas of the globe (Ash & Gallup, 2007; Kanazawa, 2008). It has also been found that latitude ($r = 0.61$) and population density ($r = 0.79$) are strongly related to cranial size, leading to the conclusion that the burden of natural selection has moved from "climactic and ecological to social" (Bailey & Geary 2009. p. 77). Food procurement is more problematic in colder climates, thus necessitating a more future-oriented frame of mind, and the more people there are in one's group, the greater the number of social relationships one must navigate. In navigating those relationships, humans slowly developed what psychologists call a theory of mind—the capacity to reason about the mental states of others with whom we interact. These relational challenges naturally lead to the selection for greater intelligence, which means more cerebral mass and bigger crania in which to house it. About two million years separate *Australopithecus afarenis* and *Homo sapiens,* and during this period, hominid cranial capacity has increased from an average of 450cc to 1350cc, which, on an evolutionary time scale, is warp speed (Adolphs,

2009). Among modern healthy humans, a large number of structural magnetic resonance imaging studies find that total brain volume (suggesting more neurons) is moderately correlated with intelligence at between r = 0.30 and 0.40 (Deary, Penke, & Johnson, 2010).

Cold Winters Theory

It is here that one contentious (some would say "incendiary") hypothesis of why race differences in intelligence (or at least in its measurement) exist appears in the form of "cold winters theory" (CWT). CWT theorizes about how different levels of intelligence evolved in different regions of the world. It asserts that colder and more seasonal climates (Northern Europe and South-East Asia) imposed higher cognitive demands for planning, particularly for the storage of food and fuel, the making of warm clothing, and the building of studier places of habitation. This reminds us of the old saying that: "Necessity is the mother of all inventions." Pesta and Poznanski (2014, p. 271) inform us that:

> CWT proposes that race differences exist because of different evolutionary pressures faced by the ancestral humans who left Africa, compared with those who remained. Ancient humans leaving Africa faced "cold winters"—significantly harsher environments that placed a natural-selection premium on higher IQ. Conversely, ancient humans remaining in Africa faced no such strong evolutionary pressure. Over relatively rapid evolutionary time, mean race differences in IQ (and other psycho-social variables) emerged.

Pesta and Poznanski (2014) set out to show that it is not necessary to posit large evolutionary time periods or geographic distances to see that temperatures affect IQ levels. They looked at predictors of average state IQ in the 48 contiguous U. S. states controlling for the percentage of Blacks and Native Americans living there, religion, crime, education, health, income, and temperature in regression models. They found that only crime (β = - 0.396) and temperature (β = - 0.399) significantly predicted IQ; that is, the higher the average state crime rates and temperature levels, the lower the average state IQ. Pesta and Poznanski were not contesting CWT; they only purported to show that evolutionary processes are not necessary for temperature and IQ to correlate meaningfully. However, higher temperatures are also correlated with higher parasite load, and as we will see, this is also a significant predictor of mean IQ across the world and within the United States (Eppig, Fincher, & Thornhill, 2010; 2011). Furthermore, a recent study (Bird, 2021) casts doubt on the CWT and suggests that the magnitude of the genetic contribution to Black–White differences in IQ is likely much smaller than it predicts.

Brain Physiology and Intelligence

A relatively simple way of defining intelligence physically is to correlate IQ scores with nerve impulses that reflect individuals' speed and accuracy in information processing in terms of reaction time (RT). The premise of RT studies is that higher-IQ people possess brains that are able to spot, differentiate, and respond to relevant stimuli faster than lower-IQ people. In other words, their neurons switch from a refractory and an excitatory state quicker. The three principal tests of RT are (in increasing difficulty): (1) Simple RT measures the time (in milliseconds) it takes someone to recognize and respond to stimuli. (2) Recognition RT involves responding to the correct stimuli while ignoring distracters. (3) Choice RT involves matching responses by pressing the letter key corresponding to the stimulus appearing on a screen while ignoring distracters. Correlations between reaction time and IQ range from - 0.25 to -0.50 (higher IQ = shorter reaction time), with the largest correlations associated with the more challenging RT tasks (Deary, 2003).

Higher correlations are found in more sophisticated measures of brain activity, such as cerebral glucose metabolism. Cerebral glucose metabolism is measured by positron emission tomography (PET) scans which reveal metabolic functioning as the brain takes up positron (anti-matter) emitting glucose. A computer is used to reveal colorized maps of the brain identifying the parts activated (mainly the lateral prefrontal cortex, which is crucial for integrating abstract relationships) while engaged in an intellectual task as the energy supplied by the glucose is metabolized. Glucose metabolic rates at various brain slice levels have been correlated with scores on the highly g-loaded Raven's Advanced Progressive Matrices. Depending on brain slice level and brain hemisphere, correlations ranging between -0.44 and -0.84 are found, which means that high IQ subjects expend less brain energy when performing intellectual tasks and possess brains that are speedier, more accurate, and more "energy efficient" than low IQ subjects (Gray & Thompson, 2004).

Further evidence for the biological substrate of intelligence is supplied by structural and functional magnetic resonance imaging (MRI) studies. A structural MRI study of monozygotic and dizygotic twins found *g* to be related to the amount of gray matter in the brain and that the amount of gray matter is highly heritable, with a mean heritability of 0.88 (Glahn, Thompson, & Blangero, 2007). Posthuma et al. (2002), among others, have shown that the association between brain volume and *g* is mediated by common genetic factors, i.e., the same genes that influence brain volume influence *g*. A twin study using structural MRI found correlations between various brain volume regions (total brain volume, neocortex white matter, and prefrontal cortex) and cognitive skills (verbal IQ, performance IQ, processing speed, and reading ability) ranging between 0.32 and 0.89 (Betjemann et al. 2010).

The most recent review of neuroimaging studies (Dizaji et al. 2021) shows that although there is no one brain area where intelligence is located, it is most likely located in a network of brain regions of the frontal and parietal lobes. Based on 37 neuroimaging studies, Jung and Haier (2007) formulated a theory of intelligence called the Parieto-Frontal Integration Theory (P-FIT). P-FIT stipulates a network of brain regions that are predominantly involved in complex reasoning and suggests that fluid intelligence is related to how efficiently information processing is shunted around the brain and how well the relevant brain areas communicate with one another. As Van den Heuvel et al. (2009, p. 7619) put it: "human intellectual performance is likely to be related to how efficiently our brain integrates information between multiple brain regions. The most pronounced effects between normalized path length and IQ were found in the frontal and parietal regions. Our findings indicate a strong positive association between the global efficiency of functional brain networks and intellectual performance." Gur et al. (2020) found additional evidence for P-Fit but noted that it should be extended by incorporating brain nodes that support motivation and affect.

Jung and Haier (2007) also assert that there is no single brain location where intelligence is situated and place their emphasis on brain areas that multiple neuroimaging studies have found to be related to IQ. Based on this information, they concluded that most of these brain areas are indeed found clustered in the frontal and parietal lobes that are connected by a bunch of curving white matter fibers called the arcuate fasciculus (Deary, Penke, & Johnson, 2010). Using fMRI with 115 children, Langeslag et al. (2013) found that higher nonverbal intelligence was associated with increased functional connectivity between the right parietal and right frontal regions. The function of these areas is to integrate sensory information, among several other things. This fits nicely with the body of research showing that the parietal-frontal network is strongly activated under situations where conflicting alternatives are possible and when response selection is required (Brass & Cramon, 2004). Resolving conflicting possibilities by making the correct selection is exactly what one engages in when taking an IQ test.

Dennis Garlick's (2002; 2003) neuroplasticity model of intelligence argues that individuals inherit different genetic set-points for brain plasticity rather than differential intelligence per se and that environmental factors then provide the necessary input to realize their intellectual potential. Garlick argues that low-IQ individuals have brains that do not adapt as well to environmental conditions as the brains of high-IQ individuals. The model posits that intelligence is "created" when neural connections in the brain are forged and strengthened by environmental input, and more or less of it will be created according to the differential capacity of individuals' neurons to adapt. Garlick argues that there is a critical period in which the developing brain fine-tunes its ability to adapt to novel phenomena. This adaptation refers to efficient signal transduction, which is attained via molecules that promote both brain development and plasticity. The primary molecules are brain-derived neurotrophic factor (BDNF), cyclic AMP response element binding protein (CREB), and extracellular signaling-related kinases. These three molecules work in concert to promote gene expression and brain plasticity (Ehrlich & Josselyn, 2016). This period of adaptation begins in infancy when the human brain is most plastic (when it is most able to make new neural connections in response to experience) and ends about mid-adolescence; i.e., when fluid intelligence is said to stop developing.

A 10-year longitudinal MRI study of more than 300 children and adolescents found strong evidence for Garlick's model. Shaw and his colleagues (2006) showed an identical pattern of brain maturation that occurred in all subjects (the cortex gets thicker, peaks, and then gets thinner with pruning), but also that the rate of these brain changes differed significantly according to IQ levels. The cortices of subjects with the highest IQs started out thinnest, quickly got thicker, peaked relatively late, and thinned very quickly. Average and below-average subjects experienced these same changes but at slower rates, suggesting that rapid brain changes reflect a high degree of neural plasticity and that greater neuroplasticity suggests a more agile mind and higher IQ. It is not all about innate biological processes, however, because these maturational processes are affected by what children experience in their environments. As Boyce and Kobor (2015, p. 15) point out:

> Environmental influences are modulated by critical periods in development, when neurobiological circuitry is especially responsive to experience and plasticity is most accessible; the opening and closing of critical and sensitive periods are regulated by epigenetic events that guide the maturation of excitatory and inhibitory neural circuitry and the expression of molecular 'brakes' that reverse the brain's inherent plasticity.

Thus, neuroscientific research confirms the central role of neural plasticity in human cognition and highlights how training, practice, and what experiences can cause structural and functional changes in the brain. While plasticity has early sensitive periods for shaping the brain, it retains a fair degree of it in later life. Studies of London taxi drivers provide compelling evidence of the brain's ability to transform itself in response to mental activity in adults. London cab drivers have to constantly learn new routes in a city of over 600 square miles with streets laid out in a spaghetti-like snarl. Taxi drivers do not only have to learn the geography of London but must use their episodic memories to improvise when confronted with traffic jams and roadworks and change routes according to the time of day, and make other strategic decisions to get their passengers where they want to go. Using fMRI scans, the researchers find that cab drivers have significantly larger hippocampi (the organs of memory) than Londoners employed in other working-class occupations, and the longer they had been employed as taxi drivers, the larger these structures are found to be (Woollett & Maguire, 2011).

The most recent development in the neuroscience of behavior, disease, and cognitive function is the Human Connectome Project (HCP). The HPC is a consortium of neuroscientists from multiple research labs in different parts of the world. It is designed to enable neuroscientists to navigate the geography of the brain by diagraming its structural and functional connectivity of the brain using every available brain imaging tool. The objective of functional network connectivity research is to characterize brain functions that can identify an individual from others, and it does so with an astounding accuracy of up to 99.5%. This as be characterized as "brain fingerprinting" in an analogous way to genetic fingerprinting via DNA profiling (Finn et al., 2015).

Finn and his colleagues (2015) looked at the connectome of 118 individuals and found that the integrity of the frontoparietal networks predicted fluid intelligence scores at r = 0.55 and concluded: "That the frontoparietal networks were most distinguishing of individuals—and the most predictive of behavior—is consistent with the role these networks play in cognition. Nodes in these networks tend to act as flexible hubs, switching connectivity patterns according to task demands" (Finn et al., 2015, p. 1669). Using data from 889 subjects, Cai et al. (2021) looked at connections in multiple brain areas and found that the frontoparietal was significantly related to fluid intelligence (r = 0.548), cognitive flexibility (r = 0.50), inhibition/executive function (r = 0.493), and language comprehension (r = 0.535).

The Role of the Environment in Brain Development

Neuroplasticity is thus the evolutionary adaptive capability to change the strength of connections between the brain's billions of neurons. It is not all about inherited biology, however. The current environment is hugely important in the development of the brain; the argument is not anymore "*whether* the environment thoroughly influences brain development, but *how* it does" (Quartz & Segnowski, 1997, p. 579). Neuroscientists distinguish between two brain developmental processes that *physically* capture environmental experiences over the organism's lifetime: experience-expected and experience-dependent (Schön & Sílven, 2007). Every human being inherits species-typical hard-wired brain structures and functions produced by a common pool of genetic material; these are the experience-expected mechanisms that reflect the phylogeny of a species' brain. Natural selection moves population traits towards genetic fixity (genetic variability is eliminated) the more important a feature becomes to survival.

Although experience-expected mechanisms are hard-wired, they require specific environmental experiences to trigger them. That is, there is an evolved neural readiness during "critical" or "sensitive" developmental periods to incorporate environmental information that is vital to an organism and which cannot be left to the vagaries of experiential learning. Evolution "recognizes" that certain processes such as sight, speech, depth perception, mobility, and sexual maturation are vital and has selected for mechanisms designed to take advantage of experiences occurring within the normal range of human environments. Pre-experiential brain organization frames our experiences so that we will respond consistently and stereotypically to them (Geary, 2005). Maturational processes will always occur "as expected" in genetically normal individuals experiencing the normal range of human environments. If individuals experience gross departures from these expected environments, such as never hearing human speech or having their eyes blindfolded at birth, there may be many negative outcomes, such as the inability to talk or to see (Twardosz & Lutzker, 2010). Of course, these experiences are so extremely rare as to be largely discounted.

Experience-dependent mechanisms reflect the brain's plasticity (Gunnar & Quevedo, 2007). Individuals will vary in brain functioning as their genes interact with the different environments they will encounter to construct those brains. That is, the wiring patterns of the brains of different individuals depend on the kinds of physical, social, and cultural environments they encounter. As Depue and Collins (1999, p. 507) wrote: "experience-dependent processes are central to understanding personality as a dynamic developmental construct that involves the collaboration of genetic and environmental influences across the lifespan." Although brain plasticity is greatest in infancy and early childhood, it is maintained to a lesser degree across the lifespan as we shape and reshape the brain (think of the London cab drivers) in ways that could never have been genetically pre-programmed. The distinction between experience-dependent and experience-expected development is best illustrated by language. The *capacity* for language is entirely genetic (a hard-wired experience-expected species-wide capacity), but what language(s) a person speaks is entirely cultural (soft-wired in experience-dependent culturally-specific fashion). The experience-expected nature of language explains why children learn (perhaps "acquire" or "develop" are better terms than "learn") language almost effortlessly as if by osmosis, while evolutionarily novel things such as calculus or chemistry are experience-dependent and are learned with some difficulty.

Synaptogenesis

The process of wiring the brain is known as *synaptogenesis*, a process that occurs both according to a genetic program and the influence of the environment. Synapses are the connections made among neurons, and the number of them made is astronomical: "The human brain has 10^{15} connections and around 100 billion neurons, so roughly as many stars as there are in the Milky Way" (DeWeerdt, 2019, p. 6). During the first few months of an infant's life, dendrites proliferate, and specialized glial cells wrap around axons to begin the process of myelination (the lipid coating around axonal strands), making for speedier transmission of electrical impulses. Dendrite growth and axon myelination continue throughout life but proceed at an explosive rate during infancy and toddlerhood. The experience-expected "lower" brain regions (spinal column and limbic regions) are the first to be myelinated, and some "higher" and most human brain regions, especially the pre-frontal cortex, are not fully myelinated until early adulthood (Sowell, et al., 2004). This is a large part of the reason why adolescents lack mature executive functioning and self-control, which are housed in the pre-frontal cortex, and exhibit so much antisocial behavior during this period of their lives (Walsh, 2009).

The birth of a set of synapses is less important than whether they will survive the competition for synaptic space. The most active period of synaptogenesis is infancy and toddlerhood, although about half of these connections will eventually be eliminated (pruned). In the earlier phases of synaptogenesis, dendrites send their feelers out to mate promiscuously. Some will be only "one-night stands, while others will establish more permanent relationships. The brain creates and eliminates synapses throughout life, but creation exceeds elimination in the first two years, after which production and elimination are roughly balanced until adolescence when elimination exceeds production (Giedd, 2004).

This process of selective production and elimination of synapses has been termed *neural Darwinism* by Nobel Prize winner Gerald Edelman (1992), who posits a selection process among competing brain modules (populations of neurons). Neuronal connections are selected for retention or elimination according to how functionally viable they prove to be in the person's environment in the same way that environmental challenges select from a population's reservoir of genetic variation in evolutionary time. The brain's neuronal populations thus evolve in somatic time, like species evolve in geological time by the selective elimination or retention of genes. Synaptic retention is a use-dependent process in which connections that are sustained are those that exchange information most frequently and most strongly (Penn, 2001). Experiences with strong emotional content are accompanied by strong electro-chemical impulses to become more sensitive and responsive to similar stimuli in the future (Shi, et al., 2004). Frequently activated neurons are thus primed to fire at lower stimulus thresholds once neurological tracks have been laid down, just like a trail in the forest becomes easier to follow the more often it is trodden. This process is summed up in the neuroscientists' saying: "The neurons that fire together wire together; those that don't won't" (Penn, 2001, p. 339).

It is thus safe to say that the neurological evidence is unequivocal on two major points about brain development: (1) the brain is always a "work in progress," and (2) its development is "use-dependent." The gene-environment interplay in the developing brain should not be forgotten when interpreting IQ data because: "The adversities inherent within environments of poverty, neglect and trauma are transduced into molecular events controlling the expression of neuroregulatory genes, which in turn guide brain development, calibrate stress reactivity, and influence lifelong risks of psychopathology and other morbidities" (Boyce & Kobor, 2015, p. 15). Boyce and Kobor (2015) explored the role of epigenetic processes in brain development; processes we briefly explore in the next chapter.

Chapter 4

Genetics and Intelligence

Behavioral Genetics and the Concept of Heritability

The social sciences have historically had a fractious relationship with genetics, deeming it "socially dangerous," "genetic determinism," or "inegalitarian." But times are changing with the deluge of genetic information gained since the completion of the Human Genome Project in 2000, and today: "sociogenomic findings are increasingly embraced by top sociology journals" (Mills & Tropf, 2020, p. 554). Yet, there are still those, especially among the older generations of social scientists, who have a misunderstanding and fear of genetics, believing that it undermines the role of the environment. I point such individuals to a statement by Baker, Bezdjian, and Raine (2006, p. 44): "The more we know about the genetics of behavior, the more important the environment appears to be."

Behavioral genetics is the study of genetic and environmental sources of trait and behavioral variations. Heritability (h^2) is a quantification ranging between 0 and 1 of the extent to which variance is attributable to genes in a particular population and is calculated via the simple formula: $h^2 = 2(rMZ - rDZ)$. That is, h^2 is twice the difference between the monozygotic (MZ) and dizygotic (DZ) twin pair correlations for a given variable. It is a *population* parameter that apportions trait variance averaged over all subjects into genetic and environmental sources, and its values depend on environmental quality. Behavioral genetics is about *variation* in traits or behavior in a particular population, in a particular place, at a particular time; they cannot inform us which genes influence our traits or behaviors, but tell us the extent to which people in a particular population differ genetically with respect to those traits and behaviors.

All cognitive, behavioral, and personality traits are heritable, which led Turkheimer (2000) to posit that $h^2 \neq 0$ be enshrined as the first law of behavioral genetics. A meta-analysis of 2,748 twin studies published over 50 years using more than 14.5 million twin pairs from 39 different countries showed that all human traits are heritable (Polderman et al., 2015). Heritability coefficients of around 0.50 have been calculated for such unlikely features as divorce and political ideology. Of course, there are no "divorce" or "political ideology" genes any more than there are "crime genes." What h^2 captures is a variety of genetic variants that, in concert with the way they interact with their environments, make an outcome more likely than not. People who are difficult to get along with, are unwilling to compromise, and/or find it difficult to remain faithful are more likely to get divorced than with the opposite traits (Hatemi, McDermott, & Eaves, 2015). It is those heritable traits that are partly genetic; not divorce per se. Likewise, our temperaments tend to make some people view the political world *primarily* through their feelings and other people *primarily* via more intellectual analysis (Walsh, 2022).

There are two ways behavioral geneticists use examine environmental and genetic influences on a trait: adoption and twin studies. Adoption studies are "natural experiments" that randomize genes (identical twins adopted into different families) to investigate the effect of shared environments and randomize environments to investigate the effect of shared genes. To the extent that genetically unrelated individuals (twins and genetically unrelated siblings) reared in the same home display trait similarities, they must be entirely a function of a shared environment, and similarities between genetically related individuals reared apart must be entirely a function of shared genes. The correlation between twin pairs reared apart is a straightforward indication of heritability since there is no shared environment, and the correlation between unrelated individuals reared in the same home is a straightforward measure of shared environment effects since they share no genes. You might object that adoption agencies try to place siblings (twins or otherwise) in similar SES homes, but as Lykken (1995) points out, the correlation between SES of placement families of adopted siblings is an average of 0.30 while the SES correlation for DZ (fraternal twins) twins reared together is a perfect 1.0.

Twin studies rely on comparisons of correlations for a trait between monozygotic (MZ; identical) twin pairs and same-sex dizygotic (DZ; fraternal) twin pairs to sort out genetic and environmental sources of trait variance. MZ twins share 100% of their genes, and DZ twins share an average of 50% of their genes. Thus, the more genes that pairs of individuals share, the more similar they should be in their phenotypic traits. Behavioral genetic studies are not perfect, but they provide unparalleled precision in studies of human personality and behavior. Purely environmental research could only achieve the same level of precision if we were to "have 'identical environmental twins' whose experiences were exactly the same, moment by moment, and another variety [DZ twins] who shared exactly but randomly [as they share randomly 50% of their genes] 50% of their experiences" (Turkheimer, 2000, p. 162). There are no such environmental twins, but they are not needed because behavior genetics informs us of the environmental contribution as surely as if there were because $1.0 - h^2$ is the proportion of phenotypic variance attributable to the environment.

Heritability is the proportion of variance in a trait attributable to *actualized* genetic potential in a population; we cannot infer from it what the unactualized potential may be. Determining heritability requires that every phenotype be exposed to identical developmental environments because variation can only be attributed to factors that vary. Lewontin (1970) illustrates this by supposing a sack of genetically *heterogenous* corn seeds planted in two plots of soil in which conditions are carefully controlled to ensure each plant receives the same nutrients. Because there is no variation in the environment, differences in height within each plot will be due entirely to genes; that is, h^2 for height will be 1.0. However, if one of the plots contains a low nitrate concentration, the corn in that plot will grow shorter on average for purely environmental reasons, even though h^2 within it will still be 1.0. Likewise, if we took genetically *homogeneous* corn seeds and planted them in diverse environments, genetic material would be constant, and phenotypic trait variance would be 100% attributable to the environment ($h^2 = 0.0$). Of course, if $h^2 = 1.0$, it does not mean that the environment is irrelevant for the trait in question because genes need an environment to actualize; then, it only means that the environment did not contribute to the *variance* in height. Similarly, if $h^2 = 0.0$, it does not mean that genes did not contribute to height. It only means that genes accounted for none of the *variance* in height, but without genes, the environment is barren. Genes provide the potential; the environment determines the extent to which that potential is actualized.

Heritability in Different Environments

Heritability coefficients are higher in advantaged than in disadvantaged environments because, like roses planted in an English garden versus the Nevada desert, advantaged environments bring out the best in the genetic material. A dramatic example of this is the average 5-inch difference in height between North and South Koreans. North and South Koreans are genetically the same people, so this gap must be attributed to their different environments. Heritability is higher among the taller South Koreans because their nutrition needs are more sufficiently met there than in North Korea, so their environment (which is more constant) is a less important component in height variation in South Korea than genes. In North Korea, access to nutritional food is far more variable, and so the environment (one's political status in the dictatorship) contributes more to height variation. Thus, the greater the environmental equality relative to the trait in question (including intelligence), the more genes contribute to it (Schwekendick, 2009).

Advantaged environments offer a greater range of opportunities for individuals to choose their path in life consistent with their desires, leading to more genetically influenced behaviors and, thus, greater heritability coefficients (Selita, & Kovas, 2019). Disadvantaged environments (poverty, single-parent, disorganized neighborhoods) have a strong influence on behavior, and consequently, genetic influences will be weaker, especially for genes associated with prosocial traits. Turkheimer et al.'s (2003) finding of h^2 values for IQ of 0.72 in advantaged environments and 0.10 in disadvantaged environments is indicative of this. Disadvantaged environments will, however, permit the expression of genes associated with antisocial traits. An individual raised in a disadvantaged environment is analogous to planting roses in a weed patch and expecting them to thrive. Prosocial traits such as altruism, honesty, and conscience need careful cultivation to grow. Antisocial traits, such as low self-control, aggression, and negative emotionality, are like weeds; a default option that will shoot up through the cracks.

Shared and Non-Shared Environment

In addition to genetic effects, behavioral genetics apportions trait variance into shared (c^2) and non-shared (e^2) environmental components. Shared environments are everything twins have in common, such as familial SES, and neighborhood, and non-shared environments are those environments unique to individual twins, such as different friends and experiences. It is invariably found shown that shared environmental effects on cognitive and personality traits in childhood disappear almost completely in adulthood, meaning that the environmental shaping of personalities is specific to individuals (e^2) rather than shared with siblings. Nielsen's (2006) longitudinal study of 1,072 American MZ and DZ twins pairs looked at verbal IQ (VIQ), grade-point average (GPA), and college plans (CPL) and partitioning the variance of all three measures into a genetic, shared environment, and non-shared environment components. Heritability for these measures ranged from 0.536 to 0.67; non-shared environment variances ranged from 0.33 to 0.37, and shared environment variances ranged from 0.002 to 0.137. The variance explained by SES (shared environment) across all measures is not significantly different from zero, but the variance explained by genes and non-shared environment is substantial.

Burt and Simons seize upon the near-zero effects of the shared environment on many facets of life to question the utility of the concept of heritability in criminology research: "Indeed, the conclusion from many of these heritability studies that little—if any—of the variance in criminal behavior is due to shared environments, often interpreted to include parenting and community factors, contradicts a wealth of research conducted during the past century as well as the major theories of crime" (2015, p. 224). The research that behavioral genetics allegedly contradicts, however, has a totally different goal. It looks at purely environmental sources of mean differences in criminal offending between demographic groups and says nothing about individual differences within them. Behavioral genetic studies showing low to zero effects of the shared environment only mean that parental effects on personality and cognitive traits that made siblings somewhat similar while they shared a home failed to survive the period of common rearing. This is not the same as saying parents or communities have no effect on the *mean* level of these features. The weak effect of shared environments in heritability studies means only that they have few *similar* effects on adult siblings for behavioral, personality, and cognitive traits; it does not mean they have had *no* effect. Environmental factors can have large effects on the mean of any number of phenotypic traits without affecting trait *variance*. The stability of genetic variance means that heritability can remain stable even while the mean level of a given variable is rising, falling, or staying the same.

Gene-Environment Interaction and Gene-Environment Correlation

Gene-environment interaction (G x E) and gene-environment correlation (rGE) emphasize the inseparability of genes and environments for human development and behavior choices. We cannot predict a developmental or behavioral outcome from either genes or environments alone; only from both in combination. We do not need geneticists to tell us that people are differentially sensitive to identical environmental influences and will respond to their environments in different ways. This is the common-sense notion underlying G x E: "The heat that melts the butter hardens the egg" (Nettler, 1984, p. 295). Children with traits such as low self-control and low fear are genetically more vulnerable to opportunities for antisocial behavior in their environment than more self-controlled and fearful children. Extroverted and sensation-seeking individuals will be attracted to careers in the military, in firefighting, or the police, while those inclined to introversion and prudence will be attracted to less exciting and dangerous occupations.

The concept of rGE is based on the notion that people seek environments that are compatible with their genetic dispositions (genes and environments will covary positively). There are three kinds of rGE: passive, evocative, and active. Passive rGE is the correlation between a child's genotype and its environment and is called "passive" because neither the child's genes nor its behavior is responsible for the correlation; rather, the correlation is the product of their parents' genotypes (Sesardic, 2003). A child who receives parental genes conducive to high intelligence will doubtless find itself in an environment in which intellectual activities are modeled and reinforced, and the opposite is also doubtless true.

Evocative rGE refers to how other people in children's environments (parents, siblings, teachers, peers) react to them on the basis of their behavior. The behavior of others towards a child is as much (perhaps even more) a function of the child's evocative behavior as it is of the interaction style of the people who react to it. The behavioral characteristics and personality traits children present to others increase or decrease the probability of evoking certain kinds of responses from others. A disrespectful and bad-tempered child will evoke fewer positive responses from others than will a good-tempered and respectful child, regardless of a parent's or teacher's own traits and characteristics. Some children may evoke such punitive reactions from others that will exacerbate their already antisocial personality and drive them to seek out others similarly predisposed ("birds of a feather"); further reinforcing their antisocial tendencies and choices. Evocative rGE thus magnifies differences among phenotypes.

Active rGE refers to the environments sought out by individuals compatible with their natures. That is, our genes nudge us in the direction of features of the social world that will be salient and rewarding to us, and we will seek them within the range of cultural freedoms and constraints. In active rGE, genes guide the individual's choice of environments which then loop back to shape and further reinforce the expression of his or her disposition. Active rGE gains more explanatory power as individuals mature and acquire the ability to take greater control of their own lives and make choices. This coheres with consistent findings that MZ twins reared apart construct their own lives about as similarly as MZ twins reared together (Carey, 2003) and that MZ twins reared apart construct their environments considerably more similarly than DZ twins raised together (Bouchard & McGue, 2003). This is reminiscent of the old adage: "The older I become, the more I become myself."

The concept of rGE alerts us to the fact that people don't just find themselves in criminogenic environments by happenstance. Even children who unfortunately find themselves in bad neighborhoods and abusive families in which they have absolutely no part in creating have inherited trait dispositions from parents (passive rGE) that may lead them to perpetuate those criminogenic environments. These environmental effects exacerbate criminogenic tendencies, but we cannot know the unique contribution of these effects unless we are able to rule out self-selection into them. Without behavioral genetic designs, criminologists cannot disentangle the causal effects of the environment from those of individual traits that lead to self-selection (Moffitt & Beckley, 2015).

The power of active rGE is evident from the fact that heritability increases for personality traits from childhood to adulthood because as twins grow up, they have more non-shared experiences, with DZ twins becoming much less similar to one another than MZ twins. Correlations between DZ pairs on many traits shrink as they gain the ability and the freedom to construct their own environments, and because DZ correlations shrink further than MZ correlations, heritability will increase. The ubiquitous finding that heritability increases with age reflect both the increasing ability of MZ twins to construct their environments similarly in accordance with their shared genes and, at the same time, the increasing freedom of DZ twins to construct their environments differently. Thus, human beings are active participants in the creation of environments that cohere with their genotypes when free to do so (Tuvblad & Baker, 2011).

Because genes affect differential *exposure* to environmental risks via active rGE and differential *susceptibility* to environmental risks via GxE, both processes always operate simultaneously and are difficult to untangle. In other words, people self-select into different environments on the basis of their genetically-driven preferences when they are able, and because they self-select them, they will be more susceptible to its influence (GxE) than will those there by happenstance. In addition to furthering our understanding of the role of genes in understanding behavior, the concepts of GxE and rGE have yielded enormous benefits to our understanding of the role of the environment in shaping behavior.

The Heritability of Intelligence

Intelligence is among the most heritable of human traits, with estimates ranging from 0.50 in childhood to 0.80 in old age (Neubauer & Fink, 2009). If genes did not contribute to variance in a trait, it would be logically and empirically impossible to calculate a heritability coefficient. Heritability estimates provide only statistical, not biological, evidence for genetic influence on a trait; i.e., it is a descriptor, not an explanation. Table 4.1 presents weighted average interclass correlations on IQ among many thousands of individuals of different kinship pairings. Most of the correlations are based on 111 behavior genetic studies of childhood and adolescent IQ by Bouchard and McGue (1981). The adult correlations are from various sources provided by Bouchard (1998). The pattern of correlations is consistent with that which would be predicted on the basis of broad polygenic inheritance; i.e., the greater the degree of genetic relatedness between pairs of individuals, the higher the correlation between their IQs.

Note that the correlations between pairs of full siblings and pairs of dizygotic twins fall dramatically from childhood to adulthood, reflecting the decreasing influence of shared environment on genetically influenced traits as we age. Conversely, the correlations between pairs of monozygotic twins, regardless of whether they were reared together or apart, remain stable from childhood to adulthood. Also note that the correlation between MZ twins reared apart (.72) is significantly larger than that between DZ twins reared together (.60). Genetic variants lead to high age-to-age IQ correlations across the lifespan, but their effects are amplified over time through G x E and rGE as people select environments correlated with their genetic propensities. This is why we see the greater heritability of IQ with age, that is, DZ correlations fall dramatically while MZ correlations remain highly stable.

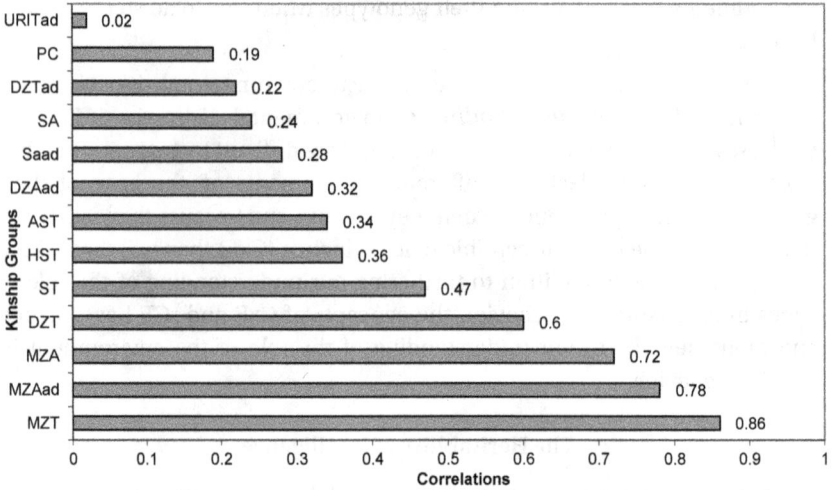

**Figure 4.1 Weighted Average Interclass IQ Correlations by Kinship Group
Source: Author Created from data supplied by Bouchard & McGue (1981) and Bouchard (1998)**

URItad = Unrelated Individuals tested as adults.   PC = Parent/adopted child. DZTad = DZ twins reared together tested as adults.   SA = Siblings reared apart. Saad = siblings reared apart tested as adults.   DZAad = DZ twins reared apart tested as adults.   AST adopted siblings reared together.   HST = Half-siblings reared together.   ST = Full siblings reared together.   DZT = DZ twins reared together.   MZA = MZ twins reared apart.   MZad = MZ twins reared apart tested as adults.   MZT = MZ twins reared together.

Molecular Genetics and Intelligence

Heritability studies tell us that genes contribute to a trait, but not which genes; we need molecular genetic studies to do this. Genes come in pairs (one from each parent) called alleles. Another word for an allele is polymorphism. There are over 14 million polymorphisms in the human genome, but only about 3% code for proteins (Jin et al., 2018). These small differences in the DNA sequence can have large phenotypic effects. The most common type of polymorphisms (about 90%) are *single nucleotide polymorphisms* (SNPs). One of the goals of genomics is to discover the actual molecular DNA underlying the traits and behavioral and disease syndromes that heritability studies tell us must be there. The ability of SNPs studied to capture all the genetic variation found in behavioral genetic studies is minimal. If SNP data account for 10% of the variance in some trait for which h^2 is consistently found to be 50%, we know that at the molecular level, we are underestimating genetic effects and need to consider more SNPs (Felson, 2014). Forero, Pereira-Morales, and Gonzalez's (2017, p. 6) review of molecular genetics and human behavior assert that the genetic contribution to human personality ranges between 30% and 50%, "of which between 15% and 37% is explained by variation in common single-nucleotide polymorphisms."

Most geneticists believe that we will eventually discover the "missing heritability" and that it is a matter of obtaining sample sizes with sufficient statistical power to identify the SNP variants using genome-wide data (Yang et al., 2015). This is a tall order since any human trait is associated with many thousands of SNPs, each with only very small effect sizes. Further complicating the effort is that each variant may affect different traits. This is known as pleiotropy or "genetic overlap;" that is, the proportion of variance that two separate traits share as a result of shared alleles. Nevertheless, the statistical gold standard for discovering these SNPs studies is the genomic-relatedness-matrix restricted maximum likelihood (GREML) method. GREML estimates heritability by examining phenotypic similarity across pairs of individuals to determine how it relates to genetic similarity controlling for covariates.

GREML studies often use samples of well over 100,000 to get sufficient statistical power, given the small effect sizes of each SNP. Significance thresholds with such large samples must greatly exceed the standard levels and are typically set at < .00000005, but even with extremely large samples, this stringent threshold captures only the largest effect sizes (Chabris et al., 2015). GREML studies have been fairly successful in finding a decent proportion of the "missing heritability." Chabris et al. (2015, p. 309) state that: "GREML studies have now confirmed that for many phenotypes, including height, intelligence, and schizophrenia, the combined additive effects of common SNPs do account for a large fraction of the variance," and that much of the heritability was not missing "but merely hiding in the form of small but additive effect sizes."

A promising quantitative predictor of heritable traits is Genome-Wide Polygenic scores (GPSs). GPSs are premised on the fact that heritable human traits are the result of the aggregated influence of a large number of common and rare SNPs. A single SNP may account for no more than 0.005% of the variance in a trait, but aggregating the minuscule effects of millions of SNPs into a GPS score allows researchers to identify individuals by their genetic propensity for traits of interest. Joo et al. (2022) conducted an impressive GPS study using data from the Wisconsin Longitudinal Study begun in 1957 and which consisted of one-third (n = 10,317) of Wisconsin high school graduates that year. The study sample was 8,527 non-Hispanic Whites, and the genetic data was 607,469 SNPs taken from participants' saliva samples. The variance of the IQ scores explained by the cognitive performance GPS was 10.4%, while impressive, it is still a long way from accounting for all the missing heritability (h^2 sets the upper limit of CPS scores). The variance of high school class rank explained by the educational attainment GPS was 17.1%. This is to be expected since educational attainment engages motivation and conscientious application, which have different SNPs underlying them, as well as raw cognitive power.

Epigenetics

The focus on gene-environment effects is shifting from genetic differences among people to gene regulation such that: "it may matter whether and to what degree a gene is transcribed and translated—and when and in what tissue—more than which allele of a gene is present" (Landecker & Panofsky, 2013, p. 349). The focus on epigenetic gene regulation in response to environmental challenges goes beyond the regulation inherent in DNA sequences to additional mechanisms not specified by those sequences. Epigenetics is defined as "any process that alters gene activity without changing the DNA sequence" (Weinhold, 2006, p. 163). Epigenetic modifications affect the ability of the DNA code to be read and translated into proteins by making the code accessible or inaccessible. DNA is only the information for manufacturing proteins; it must be transcribed and translated by other molecules in the cell if a protein is to be made.

Epigenetics is the mechanism by which our trillions of cells containing identical DNA code express different parts of it to become any of hundreds of different cell types. Epigenetic regulation of genetic activity is accomplished by two main processes: DNA methylation and histone acetylation. DNA methylation occurs when the enzyme DNA methyltransferase attaches a methyl group of atoms to a cytosine base which prevents the code from being read—no transcription order, no protein. (Carey, 2012). The opposite effect is acetylation or histone modification, which involves enzymes transferring an acetyl group of atoms that bind to the amino acid lysine tail of the histone, thus reducing lysine's attraction to the DNA's negatively charged phosphate backbone. The reduced charge loosens the chromatin enabling the gene to be activated (Renthal & Nestler, 2009). If we think of the genome as an orchestra, with genetic polymorphisms capable of producing a variety of music, then epigenetics is the conductor governing the dynamics of the performance: "The epigenetic 'conductor' controls when and what 'instruments' (genes) are to be activated and when they are to be silenced, and when they are activated, the gusto with which they may be played and what other instruments will accompany, augment, and modify the 'music' they make" (Walsh, 2009, p. 51).

Epigenetic processes may be random or caused by environmental experiences and emphasize the permeable boundaries between biology and the environment, poised as it is between the ultimate reductionism in biology (the attachment of a few atoms to a DNA strand) and that great whole we call "the environment." The genome is not a code that unfolds unerringly without environmental input like a photographic negative waiting development in the darkroom; it does not determine by itself what kind of person we will become or how intelligent we will be. As Boyce and Kobor (2015, p. 16) point out:

> [E]epigenetic processes…. comprise a broad, complex set of molecular points of connection between the experiences of early life and the proclivities, capacities and risks encoded within the individual human genome. The adversities inherent within environments of poverty, neglect and trauma are transduced into molecular events controlling the expression of neuroregulatory genes, which in turn guide brain development, calibrate stress reactivity, and influence lifelong risks of psychopathology and other morbidities. Similarly, positive early environments of nurturance, care and stability provide an anticipatory programming of many of the same genes, thereby diminishing mental health risks, optimizing neurodevelopmental preparation for learning, and ensuring normative socioemotional development.

Chapter 5

Environmental Influences on Intelligence

The Flynn Effect

Nothing has alerted us to the environmental influences on intelligence more than the Flynn Effect. The Flynn Effect refers to substantial increases in average national IQ levels due to certain changes in their cultural and physical environments. Although this phenomenon had been noted by several researchers before, it was a political scientist and psychologist James Flynn (2007) who is generally credited with systematically showing that the mean IQ (both fluid and crystallized) of the populations of all countries studied (mostly Western) has increased by an average of 21 points from 1932 to 2000. Because gene pools cannot have changed over such a short period to account for IQ changes of this magnitude, the effect has to be environmental. It should be noted that the mean IQ is still 100 because all IQ tests are repeatedly re-normalized to a mean of 100 and a standard deviation of 15 as scores increase.

These large IQ gains do not mean that our ancestors were blithering idiots. They had just as much latent intelligence as any other generation, but for most of the population, the environment was not conducive to its cultivation. According to Flynn, most people's intelligence was of a more concrete sort anchored in everyday reality. The bulk of the IQ increase has been limited to similarities ("in what way is a rabbit like a dog"), which has increased by 24 points, whereas the vocabulary, arithmetic, and information components have increased only 3 points in 55 years (Flynn, 2007). Flynn attributes the increase in similarities scores to the increasing use of "the categories of science" that has freed the mind from the concrete and allows us to understand abstractions. For instance, modern test-takers will say that both rabbits and dogs are mammals, whereas 100 years ago, an answer set in the test-takers concrete reality would more likely be that dogs are used for hunting rabbits. The largest IQ gains (and the strongest gains appear to be for fluid IQ) have been concentrated at the lower end of the IQ distribution as the environment has drastically improved to allow for more of us to realize our intellectual potential.

According to Dickens and Flynn (2001), the high heritability of IQ (strong genetic effects) coupled with large secular IQ gains (strong environmental effects) provides us with a paradox that requires reconciliation. Flynn (2007, p. 90) maintains that the direct genetic effect on IQ is only about 36%, with 64%

resulting from the indirect effects of genes interacting with the environment. The interplay of genes and environments results in what Dickens and Flynn (2001, p. 349) call the "multiplier effect." They state that "genes can get matched with environments of corresponding quality only through genetically-influenced traits." That is, a match between parents and offspring (parents provide genes and environment in passive rGE terms) results in what may be a small genetic advantage at birth being magnified ("multiplied") into a large phenotypic advantage at adulthood by a lifetime of accumulating evocative and active rGE effects on the plastic brain. In other words, genes and environments are reciprocally causative, inflating both genetic and environmental advantages in which higher IQ leads to better and healthier environments (better schools, more healthy occupational environments, higher salaries), which in turn may result in still higher IQ.

In earlier times, the multiplier effect suppressed the power of environmental effects: "The match between genes and environment means that environmental factors, however potent, to a large extent just reinforce the advantage or disadvantage that genes confer. So the match masks the potency of environmental factors" (Dickens & Flynn, 2001, p. 351). In other words, in less egalitarian times, children born into advantaged and disadvantaged environments lived in different worlds, and their accomplishments, or lack thereof, were ascribed purely to genetic advantages or disadvantages and not at all to their environmental advantages or disadvantages. Across the time that the Flynn effect has been working, the masking has slipped because of the better environments (better health care and nutrition, compensatory education, and so forth) to which successive generations of all classes have been exposed, and thus: "The potency of environmental factors stands out in bold relief" (Dickens & Flynn, 2001, p. 351).

Many cultural explanations for the Flynn effect have been offered, such as increased educational opportunities, test-wise students, changes in fertility patterns (smaller families, thus the ability to provide more resources to children), the drastic drop in the lead in gasoline, paint, and other products, and the sheer complexity of modern life. For instance, computer video games have provided a measure of mental stimulation to practically all children in modern societies that more cerebral children obtained from simply reading in the past, and even today's TV shows, according to Flynn (2007), demand more cognitive involvement than the offerings of yesteryear. In the same way that molecular genetics posits a role for numerous alleles with small effect sizes, the Flynn effect is probably caused by a combination of all of these and other environmental factors with small effects.

In terms of the increased educational opportunities as an explanation of the Flynn effect, we are confronted with another paradox in that as the population means IQ was increasing, scores on the Scholastic Aptitude Test (SAT), which is highly corrected with IQ, have been declining. How can IQ be increasing at the same time that the intellectual talents that rely on it have declined? Pietschnig and Voracek, (2015, p. 290) explain this paradox satisfactorily: "In this regard, changes in educational systems might have allowed individuals from all educational backgrounds (i.e., lower-performing individuals) to seek entry into higher education, thus explaining a rise of IQ scores in the presence of a decline of scores on the Scholastic Aptitude Test." In other words, the decline in SAT scores is attributable to the same source as the rise in IQ. That is, greater socioeconomic equality has led to more children with lower IQs taking the SAT and lowing mean SAT scores.

Richard Lynn (2009) provides the most empirically sound explanation for the Flynn effect attributable to a single variable with a large effect size. Lynn notes that the rise in IQ has been matched by a corresponding increase in the Development Quotients (DQs) of children over the same period. DQs are measured in infants by tests that assess motor (holding up the head, sitting, standing, walking, jumping) and mental development (word utterance, curiosity, naming objects, responding to questions and requests). Lynn notes that the malnutrition and mineral deficiencies that caused rickets, anemia, measles, and many other environmentally-induced problems that were still prevalent in the 1930s had all but disappeared by the 1970s in developed societies and are virtually unknown to them today. Lynn also notes that height and head size have increased during the period and that DQ is significantly related to IQ (at about $r = 0.53$ when corrected for attenuation). Lynn claims that these data rule out other proposed explanations for IQ gains, such as those mentioned above since increased DQs occur prior to exposure to these things. However, a better-prepared brain is a brain more able to take advantage of these later experiences, so the DQ data do not rule out those later experiences altogether.

Similar to Lynn's reasoning, Eppig, Fincher, and Thornhill believe that a substantial part of the Flynn effect is attributable to the huge decrease in infectious diseases in Western nations during the relevant period: "From an energetics standpoint, a developing human will have difficulty building a brain and fighting off infectious diseases at the same time, as both are very metabolically costly tasks" (Eppig, Fincher, & Thornhill, 2010, p. 1). In other words, pathogens attenuate the development of intelligence by hijacking bioenergetic resources reserved for brain development for their own growth and proliferation. These researchers found correlations between average IQ in countries worldwide and parasite stress ranging from -0.76 to -0.82; that is, the higher the parasite stress, the lower the IQ. They also found a correlation of -0.67 between the average IQ in US states and infectious disease rates in a different study (Eppig, Fincher, & Thornhill, 2011). Disease rates thus powerfully predict average national IQ, as well as average state IQs within the United States.

Woodley (2012) attempted to integrate several factors alleged to be driving the Flynn effect within the theoretical framework of life history theory (LHT). LHT is a "pace of life" (slow versus fast) theory emanating from evolutionary biology and is concerned with the strategic allocation of bioenergetic and material resources to reproductive effort across species in different environments that favor the adoption of a slow or fast life pace (Figueredo, 2006, et al.). Species that follow a slow life history live in relatively resource-abundant environments, have few and widely-spaced offspring, have low predation rates, and enjoy greater longevity than fast-paced species. Among human populations, those who adopt a slow life history (not consciously, of course) tend to live in more advantaged environments, have fewer lifetime sexual partners, and have fewer offspring later in life than fast life history individuals. In unpredictable environments with high pathogen stress and other adverse conditions, adopting a fast life history is advantageous ("Live fast, die young, and leave a beautiful corpse"). Decreased pathogen threat and decreased mortality, and longer life spans in developed nations allow for more biological energetic investment in building better brains and thus increased cognitive ability. As more advantageous environments become subconsciously encoded in the collective mind, a decreasing life history speed is encouraged in the population at large, leading to a more future-oriented populace that values education.

The End and Reversal of the Flynn Effect

The Flynn effect appears to have ended in developed nations (as well as height gains) as we have wrung all the IQ-enhancing juice out of the environment that we can (Sundet, Barlaug, & Torjussen, 2004). As we attain more equal environments, people will be more differentiated by their genes; this truism is the maddening central irony of egalitarianism. We are even witnessing a decline in mean IQ in developing countries since the high point achieved in 1998 (Flynn, 2013), although the Flynn effect is still in evidence in developing countries (Teasdale & Owen, 2008). A sample of 70 IQ experts surveyed by Rindermann, Becker, and Coyle (2016) found that most experts expected continued IQ gains in developing countries in Africa, Asia, and Latin America but a decline in Western countries. The most likely reasons given for this "anti-Flynn effect" by these experts were dysgenic fertility (low IQ individuals having more children), immigration (from low IQ countries), and declining education standards. A study covering three decades of Norwegian birth cohorts found this to be the case, at least in Norway (Bratsberg & Rogeberg, 2018). Bratsberg and Rogeberg (2018, p. 6674) note: "A negative intelligence–fertility gradient is hypothesized to have been disguised by a positive environmental Flynn effect, revealing itself in data only 'once the ceiling of the Flynn effect was reached.'"

Can we Change Individuals' IQ?

The best evidence we have for the environmental influence on intelligence is the pattern of heritability coefficients across different environments. Rowe, Jacobson, and Van den Oord (1999) and Eric Turkheimer et al. (2003) found heritability coefficients of IQ of 0.74 and 0.72, respectively, in advantaged environments and 0.26 and 0.10, respectively, in disadvantaged environments. To the extent that parents in advantaged environments encourage intellectual pursuits and parents in disadvantaged environments do not, the environmental effect on mean IQ becomes stronger between families, but genes will account for more variance in advantaged environments. However, Nisbett and his colleague's (2012) review of IQ research points out that we cannot know how much of the IQ advantage is attributable to the environment per se as opposed to the genes parents in advantaged environments provide their offspring. The gene-environment correlation effect may be evocative child-to-parent rather than passive parent-to-child in the sense that the intellectual abilities demonstrated by children ("Look at how well Jack reads" or "Look at how quickly Jill can add her numbers up") may evoke behavior from parents that result in them creating even more favorable environments that facilitate still further intellectual development. They call attention to the possibility that: "To the extent that such processes play a role, the IQ advantage of children in superior environments might be due to their own superior genes rather than to the superior environments themselves" (Nisbett et al., 2012, p. 136).

This brings up the issue of whether we can substantially increase individual IQ as opposed to average population increases. The Flynn effect is about how culture-wide environmental changes have affected *population* increases in IQ; it is not about what environmental factors affect individual IQ. The literature on individual IQ, unfortunately, reveals that it is easier to decrease than to increase latent intelligence. For instance, the Head Start Impact study, which began in 2002 with a national sample of 5,000 children, was a methodologically sound randomized control study of a public pre-K program that showed early promising results that quickly faded. In 2012, a Congressionally mandated report of the program by the United States Department of Health and Human Services (HHS) stated that the effects of: "Head Start had an impact on children's language and literacy development while children were in Head Start. These effects, albeit modest in magnitude, were found for both age cohorts during their first year of admission to the Head Start program.

However, these early effects rapidly dissipated in elementary school" (Puma et al., 2012, p. xvi).

Similar results were found in the large randomized control Tennessee Voluntary Pre-K (VPK) study. That is, positive VPK effects on achievement largely disappeared, with children in the control group catching up to the VPK children by the end of kindergarten. Lipsey, Farran, and Durkin (2018, p. 173) put it:

> Moreover, by second grade the performance of the control children surpassed that of the VPK participants on some achievement measures. This pattern was echoed on the 3rd-grade state achievement tests for the full RCT [randomized control trial] sample. VPK participants scored lower on the reading, math, and science tests than the control children with differences that were statistically significant for math and science.

Higher rates of school rule violations in later grades were also noted for the VPK children. Although these findings relate to academic achievement rather than IQ: "Educational attainment is a good proxy phenotype for cognitive performance, because cognitive performance is strongly genetically influenced and causally affects educational attainment" (Rietveld et al., 2014, p. 13791). This is not cause for surprise since intelligence and educational attainment are strongly genetically correlated (r_g=0.70) (Hill et al., 2019; Lee et al., 2018). A genetic correlation essentially means that the genes associated with one variable (in this case, intelligence) are the same ones associated with another (in this case, educational attainment).

However, there were three programs in the 1960s and 1970s—the Abecedarian, Perry Preschool, and Early Training Projects—that were concerned with raising children's IQ, among other things. Children's IQ scores increased by an average of 0.60 standard deviations, but they soon faded and then declined. Mean IQ scores at age five were 97.8, 88.9, and 91.5 for the Abecedarian, Perry, and Early Training programs, respectively. When tested at ages 14–17, the respective scores were 93.2, 80.9, and 77.7 (Anderson, 2008). Anderson claims that one positive result was higher high school graduation rates (63.9% averaged over the three studies) and that girls benefited more than boys from these programs. Of interest to criminologists, 43.3% of the Abecedarian participants acquired a criminal record in early adulthood, as did 52.8% of the Perry participants; this variable was not reported in the Early Training study.

Cofnas (2020) informs us that IQ guru Arthur Jensen was mercilessly vilified for predicting that Head Start early intervention programs that claimed we could permanently raise intelligence and academic performance would not work. He goes on to say: "If we had followed Jensen's recommendation in 1969 to devote money to programs that were tailored to the strengths of different groups rather than to Head Start, around two hundred billion dollars would have gone to improving lives instead of accomplishing nothing that can be detected" (2020, p. 139).

Factors that Decrease Latent Intelligence

There are a number of environmental factors that lead to lower cognitive functioning, which disproportionately affect African Americans. The APA report (Neisser et al., 1996) discussed in Chapter One noted that some of the differences in IQ scores between Blacks and Whites might be accounted for by such factors as childhood abuse and exposure to toxins, such as mothers drinking while pregnant and lead-based paint. Child maltreatment (emotional, physical, or sexual abuse or neglect) results in cognitive impairment, which is hypothesized to result from disruptions to normal brain development. Numerous studies worldwide have documented that maltreated children have lower IQs (see Tingberg & Nilsson, 2020, for a review). And it is noted that: "Race in the United States is a proxy for a cohort more likely to be exposed to childhood abuse, neglect, and poverty" (Sanger, 2015, p. 130).

Crozier and Barth's (2005) data from the National Study of Child and Adolescent Wellbeing showed that 32.6 % of maltreated children scored at or lower than one standard deviation below the mean on IQ (only 15.8% of children would be expected to score this low according to national norms). The Child Trends Data Bank (CTDB, 2013) reported a rate of maltreatment of 14.2 per thousand for Black children in 2012, 8.0 per thousand for White children, and 1.7 for Asian children. The rate of homicide of Black infants in 2013 was 15.8 per 100,000 and 5.4 per 100,000 for White infants (CTDB, 2014). No data were reported for Asians, but since Asians were included in all other analyses, it is possible that none occurred. Children adapt to abusive environments, but not in healthy ways. As Cozolino (2014) informs us: "We are just as capable of adapting to unhealthy environments and pathological caretakers. The resulting adaptations may help us to survive a traumatic childhood but impede healthy development later in life. . .. Because the first few years of life are a period of exuberant brain development, early experience has a disproportionate impact on the development of neural systems" (pp. xvi-xvii).

The effects of child maltreatment may be found all the way down to the molecular level, as on its effects in telomeres. Telomeres are regions of DNA at the end of our chromosomes that protect the ends from deteriorating. Telomeres fray a little each time a cell divides until they can no longer protect the integrity of the chromosome, and the cell dies. Telomere length is frequently used as a biomarker of chronic stress. Mitchell et al. (2014) used data from 9-year-old African American boys participating in the Fragile Families and

Child Wellbeing Study. They took 20 children who lived in homes with high levels of poverty, high levels of family instability, harsh parenting, and maternal depression and compared their telomere length with 20 children who lived in affluent, stable Black families who were not exposed to either harsh parenting or maternal depression. It was found that children living in the most stressful conditions had telomeres, an average of 40% shorter than those of the children living in the most nurturing settings. This is a remarkable difference given the age of the boys.

The most preventable environmental cause of low IQ is maternal ingestion of toxic chemicals while pregnant. During the process of embryonic brain development, immature neurons migrate from their birthplace to their assigned location, guided by molecular messengers. The brain is most vulnerable to insults during this migratory phase of maturation because molecular guides are susceptible to attacks by teratogens, which may send neurons to the wrong area or direct them to self-destruct (Prayer et al., 2006). The most common teratogen ingested by pregnant females is alcohol. Women who drink while pregnant introduce their fetuses to neurotoxins that produce a number of neurological disorders, the most serious of which is fetal alcohol syndrome (FAS). FAS affects the behavior of those afflicted with it via effects on the frontal lobes, amygdala, hippocampus, hypothalamus, serotonergic system, and the myelination process (Little et al., 2021).

The prevalence of fetal alcohol disorders in the United States is 1.5–2.0 cases per 1000 births (Little et al., 2021). Because heavy drinking is most prevalent among low SES individuals (Casswell, Pledger, & Hooper, 2003), FAS rates are higher among them. A review of numerous studies found the average rate of FAS was thirteen times greater in low SES families (3.4 per thousand) than in middle-class families (0.26 per thousand) (May et al., 2008). Rates of FAS per 1,000 births of all children born between 2001 and 2006 in the state of Oregon were estimated at 0.89 for Blacks, 0.26 for Whites, and 0.00 for Asians (Oregon Department of Human Services, 2002). A study by the Center for Disease Control (2002) of 437,252 children born between 1995 and 1997 in Alaska, Arizona, Colorado, and New York, found prevalence rates of 1.1 per 1,000 births for Blacks, 0.20 for Whites, and 0.00 for Asians. The zero rates for Asians reinforce the much-maligned moniker that Asians have acquired as the model minority.

Up until the early 1970s, many products, ranging from toothpaste tubes to gasoline, contained tetraethyl lead. Lead is a neurotoxin, and among its many negative effects is IQ reduction. The IQ decrement per unit increase in micrograms per deciliter of blood (μg/dl) of lead is an average of 0.50 points (Koller et al., 2004). People residing in the poorest neighborhoods and living in the oldest houses are most likely to be exposed to lead dust from paint in these old houses, the main source of lead exposure today. Toxic levels of lead (>40 μg/dl) distort enzymes, interfere with the development of the endogenous opiate system, disrupt the dopamine system, and reduce serotonin and other brain chemicals (Wright et al., 2008). An fMRI study found that grey matter was inversely correlated with mean childhood lead concentrations in mostly Black young adults taken from the longitudinal Cincinnati Lead Study (Cecil et al., 2008). The mean childhood blood lead concentration of this sample was 13.3 μg/dl. While this is well below toxic levels, it is far in excess of the 2006 average of 1.5 μg/dl in the general population (Bellinger, 2008). Although the grey matter lost to lead exposure was relatively small (about 1.2%), it was concentrated in the frontal lobes and the anterior cingulate cortex, both of which are vital behavior-moderating areas responsible for cognitive and executive functioning and mood regulation.

Lead competes with calcium for absorption, so if children do not receive adequate dietary calcium, lead tricks the body into absorbing it instead. This is important because blood lead levels are associated with a calcium absorption gene called the vitamin D receptor gene (VDR) (Mani et al., 2019). Certain polymorphisms of the VDR make the absorption of calcium more efficient, and these more efficient polymorphisms are more prevalent among people of African descent than among people of European or Asian descent (Chakraborty et al., 2008). If a variant of this gene renders calcium absorption easier, given lead's ability to mimic calcium, lead is also more easily absorbed. This creates a G x E interaction in which people of African descent absorb more lead than members of other races exposed to similar levels.

Breastfeeding: An IQ Enhancer

Breastfeeding is an experience-expected evolutionary practice and has many benefits for infants. Nutritionally, mother's milk is unsurpassed by any baby formula and provides immunologic protection against many infections via the passage of a mother's antibodies in breast milk to the infant (Jackson & Nazar, 2006). Prolonged breastfeeding is historically normative, but given the alternatives available today, it is a disappearing practice. The effect of prolonged breastfeeding on IQ was demonstrated in a large randomized study of 13,889 Belarusian breastfeeding mothers. A random half of these mothers were given incentives to prolong breastfeeding, while the other half were not. Researchers found that the children breastfed for a prolonged period of time (>6 months) had a mean IQ almost six points higher than the control group children and received higher academic ratings from teachers when they were assessed six years later (Kramer et al., 2008). The randomized experimental design allowed researchers to measure breastfeeding effects on IQ without biasing confounds such as the positive relationship between mothers' IQs and the probability of prolonged breastfeeding.

A study of 3,000 British and New Zealand children born in the early 1970s and IQ-tested in the 1990s found effects of breastfeeding on IQ similar to those found in the Belarusian study, and identified a genetic substrate (Caspi et al., 2007). It was found that subjects who were breastfed scored on average six to seven points higher on IQ tests than non-breastfed subjects. This was only true for the 90% percent of breastfed subjects who had at least one copy of the C (cytosine) base variant of the fatty acid desaturase (FADS2) gene that codes for an enzyme that converts fatty acids into polyunsaturated acids that accumulate in infant's brains in the early months after birth. These IQ gains were in evidence regardless of the social class of the mothers. There was no IQ increase noted for breastfed subjects homogenous for the less common G (guanine) base allele of the FADS2 gene. This is another example of gene-environment interaction. That is, there was no difference in the children's average IQ scores of the C versus G allele individuals whose mothers did not breastfeed them (the gene made any difference alone), and breastfeeding made no difference for individuals with two copies of the G allele.

Unfortunately, the literature consistently shows a marked downward gradient in the rates of breastfeeding as maternal IQ and SES fall. Children of lower SES and IQ women are thus more likely to be deprived of important evolutionarily experience-expected input positively associated with cognitive development. A random sample of 10,519 mothers in California found that the odds of breastfeeding for the women in the highest income category was 3.65 times the odds of the women in the lowest income category (Heck et al., 2006). Data from the Department of Health and Human Service's National Immunization Program survey (2004) reveal that in 2001 only 29.3% of Black infants were breastfeeding at six months versus 43.2% of White infants and 53.7% of Asian infants. Thus, compared with other races, Black children are disproportionately saddled with many more environmental factors known to reduce IQ.

Chapter 6

Intelligence, Temperament, and Socioeconomic Status

IQ and SES

Ever since Robert Merton (1938) wrote of American culture's overweening goal of achieving monetary success, socioeconomic status (SES) has been a central concept in sociology akin to atoms in chemistry. SES is typically measured by combining weighted measures of income, occupation, and education, and this intercorrelated matrix is viewed as an indication of success or failure in achieving the fabled "American Dream." SES is said to explain many facets of social life and individual behavior. Merton seemed to have believed that people sort themselves into his modes of adaptation based on their perceptions of their chances of achieving middle-class success legitimately. These perceptions were seen as class-linked, and the class was viewed as both given and static. That is, social class (SES) is the cause of social class; an independent variable that explains much but which itself needs no explanation other than a status that has been ascribed by an unfair society. But SES is as much a dependent variable that needs explanation as it is an independent variable that explains. The notion that SES is static implies that it is passed on to children in their parent's social DNA. However, outside of the discipline of sociology, the weak effect of parental SES on offspring SES in the United States is considered a truism: "The net impact of measured family background on economic success is easy to summarize: very little. This conclusion holds across different data sets with different model specifications and measurements and applies to both occupational status and earnings" (Kingston, 2006, p. 121).

So, what causes SES? This question is rarely addressed in the sociological literature, and for some, it is not a question we should even be asked lest it results in invidious comparisons. Lee Ellis (1996, p. 28), noting that intelligence is plainly an important factor in the three primary measures of SES—education, occupation, and income—writes: "Someday historians of social science will be astounded to find the word intelligence is usually not even mentioned in late-twentieth-century textbooks on social stratification." Merton-like sociology tends to view SES as self-perpetuating, so if offspring SES is caused by anything other than an unfair social system, it is caused by parental

SES via modeling and the transmission of values and attitudes. Any attempt to predict a person's SES from his or her parental SES, however, is hopelessly confounded by genetics. This amounts to sociological heresy, although IQ tests were specifically designed to be class-neutral measures of aptitude to turn schools into capacity-catching institutions to provide the ever-increasingly complex state and its economic machinery with competent workers (Nettle, 2003), and that is surely something to put in the plus column for IQ.

Intelligence is particularly important in technologically advanced societies in which low- complexity occupations become mechanized or moved overseas to cheaper labor markets. Postindustrial economies are incompatible with a closed caste-like society in which occupations are assigned by accident of birth. Modernization requires open competition for the choicest occupations, with class playing second fiddle to talent, the engine driving any modern economy. Employers compete for talented employees, and IQ testing has been *the* major tool used to locate them from all segments of society. Because of high training costs and high levels of failure among low-IQ recruits, the U. S. Army does not enlist anyone with an IQ below 80 (Gottfredson, 1997). Thus: "in open societies with high degrees of occupational mobility, individuals with high IQs migrate, relative to their parents, to occupations of higher SES, and individuals with lower IQs migrate to occupations of lower SES" (Bouchard & Segal, 1985, p. 408).

This was true even in the 1930s, although given the discrimination against Blacks and women back then, probably only true for White males. Ironically, the article following Merton's *Social structure and anomie* in the *American Sociological Review* examined the IQ-SES relationship (Clark & Gist, 1938) and found that they were highly correlated and that IQ served to funnel people into their various occupations of different complexity. Clark and Gist were not saying that IQ is the only cause of SES, although they did conclude that it was the most important cause. It is without question that being born into an upper- or middle-class family confers many advantages and that being born into a lower-class family brings with it many disadvantages, but those advantages and disadvantages are both genetic and environmental (Deming, 2017).

The Changing Role of Intelligence in Human History

Sociologists Adkins and Guo (2008) provide a model of the shifting role of genes in status attainment across different levels of social development across time. Using data from the *Standard Cross-Cultural Sample of the Ethnographic Atlas*, they show that the influence of genes on status attainment describes a reverse J pattern across the expanse of human historical periods. Adkins and Guo say that status differences among hunter-gathers were a function of individual traits—skilled hunter, fighter, strategist, leader, and so forth. In such societies:

"With each generation, status assortment begins on a fairly level playing field and proceeds on the basis of ability and luck. Thus, the genome→ability and ability→status relationship is apt to be relatively strong as all society members develop in largely the same environment" (Adkins & Guo, 2008, p. 248).

With the emergence of agriculture, resources became more abundant and reliable, and task specialization, private ownership of property, and social inheritance arose (Rogers, Deshpande & Feldman, 2011). With this came the possibility of the accumulation of wealth. Agriculture also brought with it large, settled populations and the need for protection against other large population groups. Protecting common group interests demanded effective leaders; that is, alpha males with all the qualities of hunter-gatherer leaders who could form kin-based coalitions. Once in place, the leader is in a position to demand surplus resources for himself and his allies commensurate with their status. Agrarian societies thus saw the reemergence of nepotism, inequality, and a dominant leadership style reminiscent of pre-Hominin primates.

The genome→ability→status relationship thus weakens as agrarian cultures become more entrenched, and only the most talented and lucky could rise above their birth station. In such cultures, status had less to do with individual traits and more to do with transmitted patterns of hereditary privilege (chiefs, aristocrats, royalty) to which others were obliged to defer. Societies characterized by huge inequalities between elites and commoners evidence a drastic reduction in the genome→ability and ability→status relationships. With the emergence of capitalism and democracy, and with reduced political, civil, and social inequality that comes with them, the genome→ability and ability→status relationship became strong again. Economic development and specialization differentiate people according to their abilities, making them more or less valuable to employers, and they are rewarded accordingly (Nolan, Richiardi, & Valenzuela, 2019).

The most ancient instincts forged in our primate history are for status and nepotism, although these natural impulses were blunted somewhat during our species' long history as foragers and hunter-/gatherers in which cooperation and equality were survival imperatives. The clash of these impulses became apparent when the trend in decreasing income inequality began to reverse in the 1970s due to shifts to a more service-oriented economy and economic globalization. According to Adkins and Guo (2008, p. 251), these shifts cast "uncertainty on the direction of future changes of the strength of genetic influence on status outcomes." For genotypes that confer exceptional phenotypic traits for achieving success in the modern workforce, the genome→ability and ability→status relationships strengthen again, but for those not so blessed, the relationship may prove disadvantageous. It is still the case, however, that, unlike the rigid caste-like societies of the past, modern "class attainments do not represent environments imposed on adults by natural events beyond their control" (Rowe, 1994, p. 136). As we have seen, genes become important to determining status in rough proportion to the equalization of environments because the more equal the access to opportunities the society provides, the greater the heritability of a trait such as IQ and personality.

Ascription versus Achievement

When considering the correlation between IQ and SES, sociologists tend to view a child's IQ to be an effect of his or her parent's SES; that is, a reified measure of class advantage or disadvantage. If this is the case, then any occupational success someone achieves that he or she claims to have meritoriously achieved is actually no more than social ascription—class of origin = class of destination. Noting that the IQs of parents and offspring are correlated (which is to be expected given genetic inheritance), Spirtes, Glymour, and Scheines (2000, p. 112) conclude that SES causes IQ: "It seems very unlikely that the child's intelligence causes the family socioeconomic status, and the only sensible interpretation is that ses causes iq, or they have a common unmeasured cause." The first clause in that sentence is so obviously true to amount to a vacuous truism, and the second clause is just as obviously untrue. As for the third clause, genes are the "unmeasured cause" they find so elusive, but if they look, they would find they are measured continually.

Plomin and Von Stumm (2018, p. 3) note this and add: "Across studies, parents' education correlates 0.30 with children's intelligence, implying that it accounts for 9% of the variance in children's intelligence. This association is, however, confounded by genetics because children inherit the DNA differences that predict their intelligence from their parents." The real test, however, is not the correlation between parental SES and children's IQ but rather the correlation between the children's IQ and their own attained adult SES. As Jensen points out that: "If SES were the cause of IQ, the correlations between adults' IQ and their attained SES would not be markedly higher than the correlation between children's IQ and their parents' SES" (1998, p. 491). Across a wide variety of studies, these correlations between adult IQ and their attained SES are in the 0.50 to 0.70 range (Jensen, 1998). Thus, the variance explained by offspring IQ in their adult-attained SES is up to four times greater than the variance in offspring IQ explained by parental SES.

DiRago and Vailant's (2007) 60-year prospective study used the original non-delinquent control male group used in the famous studies of delinquency carried out by Sheldon and Eleanor Glueck (1950). All subjects were born between 1925 and 1932 and lived in poor high-crime neighborhoods in Boston. These men were interviewed about their occupational status when they were

25, 32, 47, and 65 years of age. Attrition whittled the original 500 males in the sample down to 345 at age 65. Childhood SES was minimally statistically significantly related to occupational status (r = 0.17) at age 25, but the correlation progressively dwindled to a non-significant 0.079 at age 65. At age 65, none of the measured environmental factors were related to occupational status. Years of education (-0.410) and IQ (-0.347) were related to occupational status at age 65 (correlations are negative because occupational success was coded 1 = professional down to 7 = unskilled). These results support the behavior genetic "law" that as we age, the effects of shared environment (in this case, childhood SES, etc.) on phenotypic characteristics fade to insignificance while genes and non-shared environments become more salient.

Similarly, Nettle's (2003) study of all children born in Britain in one week in 1958, followed to the age of 42, found that childhood IQ is associated with class mobility in adulthood uniformly across all social classes of origin. Nettle found an IQ difference of 24.1 points between those who attained the professional class and those in the unskilled class, *regardless of class or origin*. He concluded that "intelligence is the strongest single factor causing class mobility in contemporary societies that has been identified" (2003, p. 560). There does remain a persistent association between class of origin and class of destination, however. In Nettle's (2003) cohort study, 39.5% remained in their father's class, but this class stability cannot all be attributed to class per se because a class of origin reflects the same genetic effects in the parental generation that class of destination does in the offspring generation (Nielsen, 2006).

Another British longitudinal study of 4,298 British males followed from age 11 to 33 (Bond & Saunders, 1999) directly tested the "class structuralist" position (the social advantages and disadvantages of childhood SES largely determine adult occupation) with the "status attainment" position (individual ability and motivation largely determine adult occupation). The study found that individual meritocratic factors (assessed when subjects were 7 years old) accounted for 48% of the variance in occupational status at age 33. All measured background variables (including parental SES) combined accounted for only 8% of the variance. Based on this 6-fold difference in the variance explained Bond and Saunders concluded that: "occupational selection in Britain appears to take place largely on meritocratic principles" (1999, p. 217). Similarly, O'Connell and Marks (2021) contrasted the power of cognitive ability and SES in a representative longitudinal study of 6,216 Irish children on academic performance. They found that cognitive ability explained much of the variance, while SES had only minor effects. None of these studies make the claim that class of origin or the family does not matter. Families obviously have lasting effects on offspring. A loving and caring family is preferable to an unloving and neglectful one, regardless of what effect it may or may not have on the offspring's IQ or any other trait.

IQ Predicts Many Outcomes in Life

In many ways, life is one continual intelligence test, with different levels predicting a variety of life outcomes besides adult SES but which are associated with it. Many are related to criminal and antisocial behavior, such as poverty, lack of education, out-of-wedlock birth, and unemployment. Many are also related to various health problems, such as substance abuse, lack of knowledge regarding how to look after one's health, and problems complying with treatment regimens. The data presented in Table 6.1 come from 12,686 White males and females in the National Longitudinal Study of Youth (NLSY). This study began in 1979 when subjects were between 14 and 17 years old, and data were collected in 1989 when the subjects were between 24 and 27 years old. The bottom 20% on IQ had scores of 87 and below, and the top 20% had scores of 113 and above. Note the large ratios between the two groups on all outcomes. For instance, for every person ever interviewed in jail or prison in the top 20% on IQ, there were 31 in the bottom 20%.

Social Behavior	IQ Level		Ratio
	Bottom 20%	Top 20%	
Dropped out of high school	66%	2%	33.0:1
Living below poverty level	48%	5%	9.6:1
Unemployed entire previous year*	64%	4%	16.0:1
Ever interviewed in jail or prison	62%	2%	31.0:1
Chronic welfare recipient	57%	2%	28.5:1
Had child out of wedlock**	52%	3%	17.3:1
*Males only **Females only			

Table 6.1 The Impact of High and Low IQ on Selected Life Outcomes
Source: NLSY data taken from various chapters in Herrnstein & Murray (1994).

To determine whether family SES background or IQ better predicts important life outcomes, Murray (2002) examined the same NLSY data and asked: "How much difference would it make to income inequality if, magically, every child in the country could be given the same advantages as the more fortunate of our children" (2002, p. 140). Murray created two samples of siblings to address this. The first was a "utopian sample" of 733 sibling pairs who were born in wedlock, had not experienced parental divorce by age 8, and whose families had a median income of \$64,586 (\$111,660 in 2022 dollars). The control sample consisted of 1,075 sibling pairs with family histories failing one or more of the criteria for inclusion in the utopian sample. Murray compared life outcomes— median family income, marital status, and out-of-wedlock childbearing— between the two samples when subjects were 30-38 years old. He also compared outcomes within each sample according to IQ levels broken down into five categories ranging from 120+ to <80. The first division compared between sample difference, and the second compared within sample differences.

The sibling pairs in the utopian sample enjoyed a considerable family SES background advantage over the control sample across each IQ category. The utopians made more money, were more likely to be married, and were less likely to have children out-of-wedlock. However, *within*-sample differences based on IQ levels were hugely greater than the differences *between* samples. The median family income in the 120+ IQ category was \$70,700 in the utopian and \$65,100 in the control sample, and \$23,600 versus \$18,400, respectively, in the < 80 IQ categories. Family SES advantage amounted to an income advantage of \$5,600 in the high-IQ category and one of \$5,200 in the low-IQ category. However, high-IQ siblings enjoyed a median income that was \$47,100 more than their low-IQ siblings in the utopian sample, and high-IQ siblings made \$46,700 more in the control sample. These data show that IQ is more important than a family background in determining income in a meritocratic society. Even if we could raise all families in this generation to the level of Murray's utopian sample, sibling differences in IQ will still produce income inequality in subsequent generations. Thus, IQ differences among siblings produce the same degree of inequality in adult income and in behavioral traits among them, as do comparable IQ differences among unrelated individuals. As Silver (2019, p. 1) states: intelligence is one of the few variables "consistently shown to influence a swath of human outcomes."

Temperament and SES

Intelligence and temperament have been called "the two great pillars of differential psychology" by Chamorro-Premuzic and Furman (2005, p. 352), who add that these two constructs are vital to predicting all kinds of life outcomes. Temperament is the template around which a person's personality is constructed, and personality aids or hinders our journey through life. It consists of a number of sub-traits such as *mood* (happy/sad), *sociability* (introverted/extraverted), *reactivity* (calm/excitable), *activity level* (high/low), and *affect* (warm/cold), all of which have heritability coefficients ranging from 0.40 to the 0.60s (Bouchard et al., 2003). Traditionally, intelligence and personality have been considered and studied as separate entities. They are separate constructs (intelligence is cognitive; personality is not), but they share some common features, particularly with respect to the Big Five personality traits. A recent large meta-analysis found correlations between IQ and personality constructs to be small to moderate but theoretically meaningful (Anglim et al., 2022). Both intelligence and personality are quite stable throughout life, both are heritable to some degree, and both are significant predictors of important life outcomes, such as SES, criminality, and health.

Intelligence is a necessary but not sufficient condition for educational and occupational success, and thus for SES. The personalities people bring with them to the workplace are certainly important. There are doubtless blue-collar workers with IQs well above the average, but just as surely, there is no one in the professional classes with an IQ below average. The average college graduate has an IQ of 115.17 (Gottfredson, 2004). Intelligence is a better predictor of what one cannot do than what one can. A person with an above-average IQ (say a little over one standard deviation, say about 120) can become a lawyer, physician, or university professor (except perhaps in the more quantitative areas such as mathematics, physics, and chemistry) if he or she is ambitious, highly motivated, and conscientious: talent + effort.

A 30-year longitudinal study of children from *middle-class* families with or without a history of temper tantrums in childhood discovered a variety of negative outcomes that can arise from a single temperamental dimension (Caspi, Bem, & Elder, 1989). The majority of bad-tempered boys ended up in lower-status occupations than their fathers, had erratic work histories, experienced more unemployment, and were more than twice as likely to be divorced by age 40 than males with more tranquil temperaments. Women with ill-tempered dispositions as children tended to marry men from classes lower than their own, were more than twice as likely as their more pleasant sisters to be divorced, had significantly more marital conflict, and were described by their husbands and children as ill-tempered mothers. This work illustrates that people with a tendency to be disagreeable and to respond more often with negative rather than positive emotionality, take their temperamental style with them wherever they go, from home to school, to work, to marriages, and that its cumulative effect can land one at the low end of the class hierarchy via erratic work histories and marital disruptions. The take-home message is that a middle-class upbringing is no guarantee of achieving middle-class status in adulthood. Individuals with bad temperaments and disagreeable lack the personal resources to move up the status hierarchy or to prevent themselves from sliding down it.

Because SES is a reflection of patterns of cognition and behavior, certain traits such as conscientiousness, agreeableness, and self-control contribute considerably to one's level of SES. Conscientiousness consists of a number of sub-traits, such as well-organized, disciplined, scrupulous, orderly, responsible, and reliable at one end of the continuum and disorganized, careless, unreliable, irresponsible, and unscrupulous at the other. Agreeableness is the tendency to be friendly, considerate, courteous, helpful, and cooperative with others. Agreeable persons tend to trust others, compromise with them, empathize with them, and aid them. This list of sub-traits suggests a high degree of concern for prosocial conformity and social desirability. Disagreeable persons simply display the opposite characteristics. Conscientiousness and agreeableness are positively correlated but far from perfectly: someone can be conscientious at work but thoroughly disagreeable as a person, and one can be most agreeable but lackadaisical at work. Thus, conscientiousness and agreeableness undergird the social skills that Deming (2017) shows are becoming ever more important in today's labor market.

Conscientiousness is more important in high-autonomy jobs such as college professor, law, and medicine than in low-autonomy jobs because it "affects motivational states and stimulates goal setting and goal commitment" (Schmidt & Hunter, 2004, p. 169). In an intergenerational study following subjects from early childhood to retirement, Judge et al. (1999) found that conscientiousness measured in childhood predicted adult occupational status ($r = 0.49$) and income ($r = 0.41$) in adulthood, which are only slightly less than the correlations between general mental ability (GMA) and the same variables ($r = 0.51$ and $r = 0.53$, respectively). Schmidt and Hunter's analysis of GMA and personality variables in attaining occupational success concluded that "the burden of prediction [of attained SES] is borne almost entirely by GMA and conscientiousness" (Schmidt & Hunter, 2004, p. 170).

Achieving high SES is a process that also requires the ability to delay gratification. Short-term rewards are easier to appreciate than long-term consequences, and thus there is a strong tendency to abandon consideration of the latter when confronted with temptation for immediate gratification. The ability to delay gratification and exercise self-control are powerful predictors of SES. The classic experiment in this area is the "marshmallow test." In this simple experiment, 600 middle-class preschoolers were told that they could eat a marshmallow placed before them immediately, or wait 15 minutes, at which time they would be rewarded with an additional marshmallow. Follow-up studies when subjects were adolescents found a number of robust correlations between delay time before succumbing to temptation (only one-third waited the full 15 minutes) and a number of outcomes associated with the social class, such as SAT verbal ($r = 0.42$) and SAT quantitative ($r = 0.57$) scores, "thinks and plans ahead" ($r = 0.36$) and "uses and respond to reason" ($r = 0.43$) (Shoda, Mischel, & Peake, 1990).

A later study of 60 of the original participants in their mid-40s showed that the ability or inability to defer gratification remained stable (Casey et al., 2011). This study brain scanned 26 of the participants using fMRI and found that high delayers more strongly activated regions in the prefrontal cortex than the more impulsive low delayers and that low delayers were more active in the ventral striatum, an area implicated in desire and reward processing. This study shows that individuals engage the interacting neurocognitive systems involved in approach and avoidance behavior—the systems of self-control—when confronted with temptation. In low delayers, the approach system is stronger, and for high delayers, the avoidance system is more vigilant.

Another longitudinal study correlated delay levels of 1,000 children between the ages of 3 and 11 years with their later life outcomes. The ability to delay gratification is a vital ability central to learning pro-social behavior, getting along with others, developing a conscience, and predicting many outcomes at age 32. Among these outcomes, the researchers looked at were substance abuse, health, the likelihood of a criminal conviction, giving birth out-of-wedlock, financial problems, and adult *SES* controlling for SES of origin and IQ. All outcomes were far more positive for those who demonstrated the ability to delay gratification as children than those who did not (Moffitt et al., 2011). Gottfredson and Hirschi (1990, p. 90) note that people low in self-control are insensitive, risk-seeking, present-oriented, and bad-tempered. The overlap among so many life outcomes shared with low IQ and low self-control suggests that these traits are related. Petkovsek and Boutwell (2014) obtained a zero-order correlation between the two traits of -0.36, and Meldrum et al. (2017), controlling for a large number of covariates, found that:

> net of all covariates, there is a significant, positive association between child intelligence during fourth grade and adolescent self-control at age 15 ($\beta = 0.15$, p b 0.001). ... What our findings suggest is that, at the phenotypic level, intelligence is associated with a greater ability to regulate one's impulses, emotions, and behavior, and may further explain why these two traits (intelligence and self-control) in general are so closely related to important life outcomes such as success in primary and secondary education, economic achievement, and avoiding contact with the criminal justice system (pp. 6-7).

These and many hundreds of other studies show conclusively that the attainment of adult levels of SES depend almost exclusively on heritable differences of intelligence and temperament and that childhood SES explains very little beyond the parental genetic transmission of these traits. It is scientific malfeasance for sociologists who continue to deny the role of genetically transmitted individual differences in the attainment of SES, one of their central concepts. The only thing that could account for why an intelligent and conscientious individual failed to achieve solid middle-class status would be a catastrophic illness or injury preventing his or her participation in the workforce.

Chapter 7

Intelligence and Physical
and Mental Health

Cognitive Epidemiology

Hippocrates, the father of medicine, once wrote: "A wise man ought to realize that health is his most valuable possession and learn how to treat his illnesses by his own judgment" (in Basmajian, 1985, p. 84). Hippocrates is thus laying much of the responsibility for health at the doorstep of the individual. We saw in chapter five that various health-related factors such as abuse, pathogen load, lead exposure, maternal alcohol and drug ingestion (negative), and breastfeeding (positive) have an impact on offspring IQ levels. That is, given exposure to harmful factors in the earliest time of life leads to lower childhood IQ. In this chapter, we look at the relationship the other way around; that is, how IQ impacts the health of individuals. Although lower IQ leads to poorer health, there is no neat linear chain of causation from intelligence to health outcomes that have yet to emerge fully. However, Linda Gottfredson (2004) maintains that psychometric g is the "fundamental explanatory paradigm." The investigation of the IQ-health relationship is known as cognitive epidemiology.

The typical research methodology of cognitive epidemiology is to obtain childhood IQ test scores and statistically analyze them in relationship with adult physical and mental illness and mortality. The core hypothesis of this research paradigm is that childhood intelligence predicts adult health and does so even in countries with universal access to free quality health care (at the point of service) and even after statistically adjusting for other important variables such as childhood SES. In short, virtually all indicators of physical and mental health favor people of higher socioeconomic status, which is assumed to be mostly a function of their higher cognitive abilities. As Lynch et al. (2004, p. 9) put it: "Every step up the socioeconomic ladder is generally associated with an increment—albeit a diminishing one—in better health."

Why might this relationship exist? Health psychologist Shelly Taylor puts the matter rather bluntly: "Factors that influence patients' ability to understand and retain information about their condition include intelligence and experience with the disorder. Some patients are not intelligent enough to understand even simple information about their case, and so even the clearest explanation falls on deaf ears" (1991, p. 310). Taylor's opinion is not without empirical evidence, however. For instance, Williams et al. (1995) found that among 2,659 outpatients of two city hospitals, 26% of them were unable to understand from their appointment slips when their next appointment was scheduled, 42% could not understand directions for taking their medication, and 59.5% could not understand the standard informed consent form. And as Dobson and her colleagues (2017, p. 238) also put it: "Individuals who are aware and understand the consequences of poor health choices are less likely to make them. If an individual is unaware of how to properly take medication, read a nutrition label, when to visit doctors, or access resources to help change their health behaviours, it can also affect the onset of CVD [cardiovascular disease] events." The inability to function effectively in a healthcare environment is doubtless embarrassing, but it can also result in very deleterious treatment outcomes or even death if people do not properly understand their diagnosis and their treatment regimens.

Scholars who find their home in the sociological tradition are generally happier the further they are from individual explanations and will thus tend to disdain Hippocrates' opinion about individual responsibility for one's health. For instance, Richard Wilkinson views focusing on people's intelligence and the choices they make as blaming the victim and thus absolves the social structure of blame. "Apart from suggested explanations of health inequalities in terms of genetics and selective social mobility, another approach, which incidentally also served to absolve the social structure of responsibility, was to imply that they resulted from differences in people's willingness to adopt a healthy lifestyle" (Wilkinson, 2002, p. 63). Intelligence and individual choices thus play second fiddle (if they play at all) to a mindless social structure that must take the blame. Wilkinson never once invoked the role of intelligence in relation to health outcomes. His disdain for intelligence as an explanation for anything at all is seen when he wants to: "caution people against taking the relationship between measures of mental ability in childhood and achieved social mobility in adult life as evidence that social mobility is a reflection of innate intelligence" (p. 204).

Health and Income Inequality

Wilkinson's solution to health disparities is a more cohesive and just society. Who wouldn't want that? But as always, the devil is in the details. What Wilkinson recommends is the redistribution of wealth, but the passing of wealth down the SES ladder does not seem to have done much good in terms of reducing poverty in this country. The United States spent around $23 trillion on Lyndon Johnson's "war on poverty" between 1964 and 2019, but as late as

2014, the economic poverty rate was about the same as it was in 1964 at about 14% (Tanner, 2019). The perennial complaint among scholars on the left is that the wealthy do not pay their fair share of taxes is far from the truth; where do they think that $23 trillion came from? It didn't fall like manna from heaven. The 2019 IRS tax data show that the top 1% of people in the US population paid 40.1% of all income taxes. How much more would the envious have them pay? The top 10% paid 71.4% of all income taxes, and the top 50% of income earners paid 97.1%. The bottom 50% paid the remaining 2.9%, and the bottom 20% of income earners have negative tax rates, meaning that they get more money back from the government in the form of refundable tax credits than they pay in taxes. People with gross incomes above $250,000 in 2018 (2.4% of the population) paid 48.9% of all individual income taxes in The United States (York, 2021). If that envied and resented 2.4% ever abandoned the United States, the economic lights would go out.

Some scholars have argued that the direction of the relationship is one in which poor health has the effect of lowering intelligence. Poor health may adversely affect intelligence, but the vast majority of cognitive epidemiological studies have looked at intelligence in childhood when poor health is a lot less frequent, and thus poor health is an unlikely cause of below-average intelligence. Of course, as already stated, fetuses, infants, and children exposed to early biological insults will suffer lower intelligence. However, it remains an article of faith for some that income inequality is the major factor that accounts for the poor health of those of lower SES due to those people lacking access to proper medical attention. Yet, it has been said that, at least in the United Kingdom, the "evidence for a correlation between income inequality and the health of the population is slowly dissipating" (Mackenbach, 2002, p. 2). After reviewing 98 studies on income inequality and health the matter, Lynch et al. (2004, p. 5) similarly concluded: "Overall, there seems to be little support for the idea that income inequality is a major, generalizable determinant of population health differences within or between rich countries."

Linda Gottfredson (2004, p. 174) takes note of the various studies of social class and health and refers to the fact that health demographers find them puzzling and paradoxical: "leading them to speculate that SES creates health inequality via some yet-to-be-identified, highly generalizable 'fundamental cause.'" She adds:

> Conventional theories of social inequality posit that social class disparities in health result from disparities in material resources, such as access to medical care. Health demographers have become increasingly puzzled, however, by certain glaring failures of the poverty paradigm. The chief puzzle is why the relation between social class and

health is so remarkably general across diverse times, places, and diseases and despite improvements in health care. In fact, greater equalization of health care and falling rates of morbidity and mortality tend to widen social class differences in health. Such paradoxes have led health demographers to posit some highly general and enduring— but still mysterious—fundamental cause of health inequalities that transcends the particulars of time, place, disease, material advantage, and social change (2004, p. 174).

The overall conclusion of the issue of income inequality and health is that greater access to medical care has made surprisingly little difference in SES differences in health. When Medicaid and Medicare were introduced in the United States in the 1960s, it led to poor people making as many visits to a physician per year as the nonpoor. However, large class differentials in health continued to be observed even when the poor began to visit physicians at a higher rate than the nonpoor (Rundall & Wheeler, 1979). Gottfredson notes that: "Great Britain and other countries that had expected to break the link between class and health by providing universal health care were dismayed when the disparities in health not only failed to shrink but even grew" (Gottfredson, 2004, p. 181). In other words, greater equalization of health care tends to expand social class differences in health rather than contract them.

Intelligence Versus SES in Various Health Outcomes and Mortality

Gottfredson informs us that there are few studies (although they are growing in number each year) that directly examine the intelligence-health relationship relative to those that examine health in relation to SES. However, she notes that SES is an excellent proxy for IQ (as has been shown in previous chapters of this book) because the usual indicators of SES (education attainment, occupation, and income) correlate robustly with each other and with total SES. She notes that years of education correlate 0.68 with IQ, and occupation and income correlate with IQ at 0.50 and 0.35, respectively (2004, p. 185). A more recent study by Christina Wraw and her colleagues (2015, p. 25) from a nationally representative sample found the correlations with IQ to be 0.64 for adult SES, 0.60 for education, 0.47 for occupational status, and 0.47 for income. It is also noted by Hill et al. (2017, p. 2) that "Both education and household income are strongly genetically correlated with intelligence, at $rg = 0.73$ and $rg = 0.70$ respectively." Again, a genetic correlation identifies single nucleotide polymorphisms that are common to two or more phenotypical traits in people.

Turning first to mortality, Steenland, Henley, and Thun (2002) looked at deaths from all causes and cause-specific death rates by educational status among the American Cancer Society cohort of 1,051,038 men and women from

1959 and formed a second cohort consisting of 1,184,657 men and women from 1982. Although IQ information was not included in the study, we know that educational attainment is strongly correlated with IQ, thus making it a robust proxy for IQ. They found that low education was associated with higher death rates in both cohorts from all causes and for most specific causes, except breast cancer and external causes (accidents, homicides, etc.) among women (breast cancer incidence is higher among the better-educated, presumably because of their reproductive patterns; that is, they have fewer children and older maternal age at first birth (Medina et al., 2022). Life expectancy for the least educated was 4.8 years shorter for men and 2.7 years shorter for women versus the most educated. Steenland, Henley, and Thun (2002, p.11) note that "The inverse relation between education and mortality was strongest for coronary heart disease, lung cancer, diabetes, and chronic obstructive pulmonary disease; moderate for colorectal cancer, external causes (men only), and stroke; weak for prostate cancer; and reversed for external causes among women."

Catherine Calvin and her colleagues (2011) reviewed and meta-analyzed the relationship between IQ (measured in youth and sometimes using different measures of cognitive ability) and all-cause mortality in 16 longitudinal cohort studies from five countries: the United States, the United Kingdom, Sweden, and Denmark (n = 1,107,022 participants). Of that number, there were 22,453 deaths. They found that a one standard deviation advantage in IQ test scores was associated with a 24% lower risk of death during follow-up periods of between 17 and 69 years. Controlling for childhood SES essentially had no effect on the magnitude of the relationship, but controlling for Adult SES reduced the relationship by 33%, which is to be expected since cognitive ability and SES overlap, but not completely. The researchers conclude with remarks regarding the presumed factors that mediate the relationship between cognitive ability and health:

> Premorbid cognitive ability may act via occupational status and wealth to reduce the risk of mortality, by providing a less hazardous work environment, a safer and more comfortable home environment, and the material means to access better and more immediate medical care. Furthermore, intelligence may be mediated by education to reduce the likelihood of death, perhaps by increasing a person's receptivity to health education messages (thereby reducing negative behaviours such as smoking and excess alcohol consumption, and promoting exercise and healthy eating), and by improving comprehension of medical terminology and instruction that impacts on disease management and prevention (2011, p. 640).

Christina Wraw and her colleagues (2015) investigated the link between intelligence tested in youth and both childhood and adult SES and health and mortality in later life among 5,793 participants in the 1979 cohort of the National Longitudinal Study of Youth. (Parenthetically, they found that IQ tested in youth was associated with adult SES at 0.64). A number of specific health outcomes were examined when participants were 50 years old. Altogether, 16 health outcomes were examined: two summary measures (physical health and functional limitation), nine medically diagnosed illnesses, four self-reported conditions, and a measure of general health status. They found that higher intelligence is linked with better physical health at age 50 and a lower risk for a number of chronic health conditions. For example, a 15-point higher score in IQ was significantly associated with increased odds of having good, very good, or excellent health. Thirteen of the illnesses were significantly and negatively associated with IQ. Controlling for SES partially mediated the relationship for a number of examined health conditions.

Marius Wrulich and his colleagues (2014) investigated the effects of fluid intelligence and crystallized intelligence on various health outcomes in a longitudinal study of a nationally representative sample of 717 Luxembourgers. Intelligence and socioeconomic status were measured at age 12, and physical, functional, and subjective health were assessed 40 years later when subjects were 52 years old. Physical health was measured by the number of visits to a physician in the last 3 months, the number of sick leave days in the last 12 months, and the number of nights spent in the hospital in the last year. Functional health was self-assessed by asking: "Looking back over the past 2 years, how much did your health status hinder the following activities?" It was found that individuals with higher general and particularly higher fluid intelligence had reported significantly fewer doctor visits and better functional health in adulthood. Crystallized intelligence had no statistically significant effects. The effect sizes for intelligence were considerably higher than those for childhood SES. Adult SES was not included in the study. It was concluded: "Childhood intelligence incrementally predicts various dimensions of adult health across 40 years— even in a country in which all citizens are guaranteed access to high-quality health care" (2014, p. 292).

Cardiovascular Health

Space constraints dictate that we limit the review of physical health problems to the most serious. Cardiovascular diseases have been shown to be the leading cause of death from chronic disease in the United States and worldwide (Schultz et al., 2018). These diseases are largely preventable and manageable (not smoking, exercising, and having a healthy diet) if one pays attention to medical advice. Paying attention, understanding, and adhering to such advice (health literacy) is presumably a function of intelligence. Socioeconomic factors must also play a part because it costs money to buy exercise equipment, join a gym, or enjoy a healthy diet. One of my own studies (Walsh, 1998) found SES to be negative and significant to blood pressure levels and hypertension, but IQ was not included in the study. Religious commitment was the factor most strongly related to blood pressure (church attenders and a measure of commitment to one's faith evidenced lower blood pressure), but that was also negatively and significantly related to blood pressure levels. SES thus matters, but studies show unequivocally that intelligence (IQ) is the more powerful predictor.

Hart and colleagues (2004) investigated the influence of childhood IQ on the relationships between various risk factors and cardiovascular disease, coronary heart disease, and stroke in adulthood among 938 Scottish participants who took an IQ test in school in 1932 when they were children. Data on cardiovascular risk factors (blood pressure, smoking, and so forth) were collected from a questionnaire and from a screening examination. Participants were followed up for 25 years for hospital admissions and death. IQ was negatively correlated with diastolic and systolic blood pressure and positively correlated with height and respiratory function in adulthood. For each incidence of cardiovascular disease, coronary heart disease, or stroke that resulted in either hospital admission or death, there was an increased rate as IQ levels decreased. The researchers noted that the effects of social factors were minimal after the effects of IQ were controlled for:

> in view of the minimal effect of social factors seen once childhood IQ was adjusted for, childhood IQ is a proxy that captures socio-economic disadvantage, health behaviours and environmental exposures more completely than other more conventional socio-economic indices in a situation where it is the combination of many factors, rather than any individual factor conferring major risk, that is important (2004, p. 2136)

There are hundreds of studies that investigate the relationship between cardiovascular diseases and intelligence, and all that I have seen show an inverse relationship. Only one of the most recent others is addressed here. Yang and colleagues (2022) examined 121 single nucleotide polymorphisms to estimate genetic correlations with intelligence and coronary artery disease (n = 184,305) and myocardial infarction (n = 171,875). All subjects were Chinese nationals. The researchers found that genetically predicted higher intelligence was significantly associated with a lower risk of coronary artery disease (OR = 0.76) and myocardial infarction (OR = 0.78) independent of confounders. The first odds ratio indicates that higher intelligence results in a 24% reduction in the risk of having coronary artery disease, and the second odds ratio indicates that higher intelligence results in a 22% reduction in the risk of myocardial infarction.

Intelligence, Mental Health, and Substance Abuse

Lower intelligence is a risk factor for a wide range of mental disorders and for alcohol and drug abuse. The public health and financial burden associated with mental health and substance abuse are enormous. O'Connell, Boat, and Warner (2009, p. 242) report that the financial cost to society of mental, emotional, and behavioral disorders was estimated in 2007 to be $247 billion ($362.7 billion in 2022 dollars). A 2004 estimate of the cost of drug abuse from the National Drug Control Policy (2004) was $165.1 billion ($244 billion in 2022 dollars), and for alcohol abuse, it was estimated at $158 billion in 1998 ($290.2 billion in 2022 dollars). These costs include treatment costs, lost production, wages, taxes, and criminal justice costs. Adding up those costs in 2022 dollars comes to a whopping $896.9 billion.

Sjölund, Allebeck, and Hemmingsson (2012) looked at data from 49,321 men conscripted for military service in the Swedish military in 1969/70. They found that IQ had an inverse and graded association with later alcohol-related problems. For alcohol-related hospital admissions, the crude hazard ratio was 1.29, and for alcohol-related mortality, it was 1.21 for every one-point decrease on the nine-point IQ scale. Adjustment for risk factors measured at age 18 attenuated the association somewhat for both outcomes. The hazard ratio is the ratio of the chance of something occurring in one group (the so-called treatment group) versus the chance of it occurring in the so-called control group at a given interval of time. A hazard ratio of 2.0 indicates that the treatment group is twice the risk of the event occurring versus the control group. In this case, the hazard ratio of 1.29, means that each point decrease in IQ score on the nine-level scale resulted in a 29% greater likelihood of receiving an alcohol-related diagnosis in the hospital. Controlling for "social position" (SES) only reduced the hazard ratio to 1.28. The researcher noted: "Our conclusion supports the suggested pathway of high cognitive abilities leading to a socio-economic position, which determines the [lower] risk for acquiring an alcohol-related diagnosis" (2012, p. 95).

Gigi et al. (2014) compared the social and clinical characteristics of 76,962 17-year-old males with borderline intellectual functioning (IQ between 71 and 84) with 96,580 17 years old males with average IQ on their social functioning, psychiatric diagnoses and drug abuse using conscript testing data from the Israeli military. They found that the borderline intellectual functioning group had higher rates of poor social functioning compared to the control group (OR =1.90), more likely to have a psychiatric diagnosis (OR = 2.37), was more likely to be diagnosed with anti-social personality disorder (OR = 3.78), and was more likely to use drugs (OR = 1.2).

Katherine Keyes and her colleagues (2017, p. 183) looked at data involving a variety of psychiatric and behavioral disorders from a nationally representative sample of 10,073 US adolescents with an average age of 15.2 years in relation to their scores on fluid intelligence. Controlling for parental educational attainment and income, they found that:

> past-year bipolar disorder, disruptive behavior disorders, and substance abuse were most strongly associated with low fluid intelligence. Lower IQ has been documented among youths with these disorders in clinical samples. Our population estimates indicate that mean IQ was approximately one-third of a standard deviation (approximately 5 points) lower than average among youths with bipolar disorder, behavior disorders, and substance abuse. The associations of behavior disorders with IQ were stronger for current disorders than for disorders that had remitted.

Note that although statistically significant, the results are not strong, and the stronger link with current disorders rather than remitted disorders cannot be interpreted to say that the disorders led to lower IQ scores because IQ was assessed premorbid. The stronger link with current disorders suggests that lower IQ is associated with chronic psychiatric disorders rather than transient disorders.

Catherine Gale and her colleagues (2010) used data from 1,049,663 Swedish men born between 1950 and 1976 who took tests of intelligence on conscription into military service and were followed up for hospital admissions for mental disorders for a mean number of 22.6 years. All conscripts took the military service conscription examination involving a structured medical assessment of physical health, mental health, and cognitive functioning. Full-scale IQ was divided into nine categories, from lowest to highest. The researchers found that the risk of hospital admission for all categories of disorder rose with each point decrease in the nine-point IQ score over the 22.6 follow-up period. They also found that for a standard deviation decrease in IQ, age-adjusted hazard ratios were 1.60 for schizophrenia, 1.49 for other non-affective psychoses, 1.50 for mood disorders, 1.51 for neurotic disorders, 1.60 for adjustment disorders, 1.75 for personality disorders, 1.75 for alcohol-related, and 1.85 for other substance use disorders. Lower intelligence was also associated with higher comorbidity of disorders. The associations changed only minimally with adjustments for potential confounders such as parental SES.

In conclusion, we must be aware of a number of possible pathways, from low intelligence to the various disorders we have looked at. The most obvious pathway is between IQ and educational attainment. Higher education brings greater access to health information and a greater readiness to live in conformity with it; that is, what to avoid (smoking, overeating, substance abuse, and other imprudent behaviors) and what to avoid (the opposites of these behaviors). Lower intelligence leads to discounting the value of more desirable delayed rewards in favor of immediate gratification. Higher education often leads to more professional occupations that generally place people in healthier work environments (not to mention higher income). Lower cognitive function is also related to intentional self-injury, accidental injury, and assaults by others, which tends to suggest an impulsive and careless lifestyle and the inability to correctly assess environmental challenges among people with low IQ (Deary, Weiss, & Batty, 2010).

The association of intelligence with so many adverse life outcomes strongly recommends that public policy be aimed at eliminating or reducing those perinatal events and deprivations examined in chapter five that result in brain insults that reduce a child's IQ and put them at risk for many other problems. Intelligence may be largely genetically determined, but as we have seen, environmental experiences have an effect on how genes are expressed, and the environment itself (e.g., the Flynn Effect and pathogen load) can independently affect IQ scores. Policies that increase IQ (or at least that prevent IQ decrement), if implemented, would result in enormous benefits to society. They would be very costly to implement, but surely the proactive cost would be well below the multiple billions of dollars that we now incur reacting to the problem of low IQ. Of course, the emotional cost of waiting until a problem manifests itself is incalculable.

Chapter 8

The IQ-Criminality Relationship

The Intelligence-Crime Relationship

The relationship between intelligence and the various life outcomes examined so far directly affect only individuals and their families, but its link with criminal behavior potentially affects us all. One of the earliest works emphasizing low intelligence as a crime risk was Richard Dugdale's "*The Jukes*": *A Study of Crime, Pauperism, Disease, and Heredity* (1877/1895). Dugdale studied the lineage of a rural upstate New York family known for its criminal activity, to which he gave the fictitious name of "Jukes." He traced the family lineage to a colonial-era character named "Max," whose descendants remained in relative isolation and largely propagated themselves through intermarriage. Dugdale eventually traced 1,200 of Max's descendants, among whom he found numerous cases of crime, disease, feeblemindedness, sexual promiscuity, pauperism, and prostitution. Dugdale's work was widely interpreted as evidence of the hereditary nature of criminality, although Dugdale himself believed that moral education could override biological propensities.

Another early study was Henry Goddard's *The Kallikak Family: A Study in the Heredity of Feeble-mindedness* (1912). This study traced two family lineages of a Revolutionary War soldier named Martin Kallikak Sr, who dallied with a "feebleminded tavern girl" with whom he fathered a son. From this lineage, there issued a variety of individuals of unsavory character. Martin then righted his moral ship and sired another lineage with a woman from a "good Quaker family" whom he married, and from whose lineage there emerged a number of prominent people and very few of unsavory character. From these two families with a common male ancestor and two female ancestors, one "defective" and the other "respectable," he concluded that "degeneracy" was the result of "bad blood" (1931, p. 69). In Goddard's (1914) book, *Feeblemindedness*, he argued that "at least 50 percent of all criminals are mentally defective" (p. 9).

Other early works hint at the role of intelligence without explicitly using the term, opting instead for words such as "talented," "untalented," or "capability." For instance, Durkheim viewed humans as similar in their "essential qualities" but realized that "One sort of heredity will always exist, that of natural talent" (1951, p. 251). Thus, although everyone is more or less equal in their natural desires, not everyone is equally capable of achieving them. Early extensions of

Merton's anomie theory by Cohen (1955) and Cloward and Ohlin (1960) noted that the individual's inability to pursue the legitimate means of attaining middle-class success as causes of crime and delinquency as much as sociocultural barriers. Cloward and Ohlin (1960, p. 96) wrote of the inability of lower-class youths to defer gratification, their impulsivity and sensation-seeking, and their preference for "big cars," "flashy clothes," and "swell dames." Writing about the status frustration lower-class youths experience, Cohen (1955, p. 66) states that these youths come to define as meritorious "the characteristics they *do* possess, the kinds of conduct of which they *are* capable." And as Vold, Bernard, and Snipes (1998, p. 177) remark: "It is not merely a matter of talented individuals confronted with inferior schools and discriminatory hiring practices. Rather, a good deal of research indicates that many delinquents and criminals are untalented individuals who cannot compete effectively in complex industrial societies."

We many dismiss these early works as exaggerations, but a number of recent reviews of the IQ/crime relationship find it to be robust, although not to Goddard's plainly inflated level (Ellis & Walsh, 2003; Farrington & Welsh, 2007; Lynn, Fuerst, & Kirkegaard, 2018). Ellis and Walsh (2003) note a study of Texas inmates that showed approximately 23% of the inmates scored below 80, and only 9.6% scoring 110 or above. By way of contrast, only 9.2% of the general population score at or below 80, and 25% have an IQ of 110 and above. The IQ-offending relationship is stronger than often indicated because most studies tend to lump together boys who commit only minor delinquent acts during their teenage years with boys who will continue to seriously and frequently offend into adulthood. Casual and less serious offending (which is relatively common among adolescents) differ from non-offenders by only about one point, while serious, persistent offenders differ from non-offenders by about 17 points (Gatzke-Kopp et al., 2002; Moffitt, 1993). Pooling these two groups hides the magnitude of IQ differences between minor offenders and serious offenders if the latter have lower IQs than the former. Lower IQ individuals tend to have an earlier onset of offending and longer criminal careers (McGloin & Pratt, 2003; Piquero & White, 2003).

Frisell, Pawitan, and Långström (2012) examined the Swedish military's Conscript Register for the period between 1980 and 1993 and violent criminal convictions in Sweden's Crime Register among 700,514 men. They also studied the relationship between IQ at age 18 obtained from the Conscript Register and criminal arrests and convictions. The most salient finding was: "Men convicted of violent crime had more than a standard deviation lower cognitive ability than those without such convictions. Beyond the discussion of a potential causal effect of lower cognitive ability on violent offending, this is clear evidence that violent individuals managed in courts, prison and probation, and forensic psychiatric services, on average, have weaker cognitive resources" (2012, p. 6). Schwartz et al. (2015) examined a Finnish birth cohort of boys (n = 21,513) born in 1987 using official criminal convictions and IQ tests administered by the military upon their conscription. They concluded:

> The clearest takeaway from this research is that low intelligence is a strong and consistent correlate of criminal offending. For example, the risk of acquiring a felony conviction by age 21 is nearly four times (3.6) higher among those in the three lowest categories (1–3) of total intelligence as compared to those scoring in the top three categories (7–9). ... cognitive ability is an important correlate of individual differences in criminal offending, a finding that criminological theories ignore at their own peril (p. 115).

Likewise, Moffitt et al. (1981) studied 4,552 Danish army draftees on IQ and criminal records drawn from the Danish National Police Register and found that men who committed two or more criminal offenses by age 20 had IQ scores averaging one full standard deviation below nonoffenders. More recently, Jacob, Haro, and Koyanagi (2019) studied a British national representative sample of 6,872 individuals and found that after controlling for age, sex, and race/ethnicity, the proportion of violent perpetrators increased monotonically going from people with IQ scores of 70-79 to those with IQs of 120–129. The lowest IQ group had 2.29 times higher odds of violent offending. There is no such thing as immaculate data in the social sciences, but verified arrests/convictions and IQ tests are about as reliable and valid as it gets.

Intellectual Imbalance

Just as pooling serious and frequent offenders with minor and infrequent offenders leads to an underestimation of the IQ/antisocial behavior relationship, so does pooling the two subscales of the IQ test. David Wechsler's (1958, p. 176) statement that: "The most outstanding feature of the sociopath's test profile is the systematic high score on the performance as opposed to the verbal part of the scale" sparked another way of examining the relationship between IQ and antisocial behavior. Most IQ studies look at full-scale IQ (FSIQ), which is obtained by averaging the scores on verbal (VIQ) and performance (PIQ) IQ sub-scales. While most people have VIQ and PIQ scores that closely match, criminal offender populations are almost always found to have significantly lower than average VIQ scores, but not significantly lower PIQ scores, than non-offenders. This PIQ>VIQ discrepancy is called *intellectual imbalance.*

As Miller (1987, p. 120) notes: "This PIQ>VIQ relationship [is] found across studies, despite variations in age, sex, race, setting, and form of the Wechsler scale administered, as well in differences in criteria for delinquency." Isen's (2010) meta-analysis of 131 PIQ > VIQ-antisocial behavior studies found that averaged across studies, VIQ was 85.9, and the average PIQ score was 93. Thus, offenders score only 7 points below the general population average on PIQ but 14.1 points below average on VIQ. The PIQ > VIQ profile was in evidence for both male and female offenders, but more so among White than Black offenders. A literature review found that overall, VIQ>PIQ boys are underrepresented in delinquent populations by a factor of about 2.6, and PIQ>VIQ boys are overrepresented by a factor of about 2.2 (Walsh, 2003). Thus, P>V boys are almost 5 times more likely to appear in delinquent samples than V>P boys. The research on intellectual imbalance provides another example of how the role of IQ in understanding criminal behavior may be underestimated if we rely solely on full-scale IQ rather than looking deeper into the effects of PIQ>VIQ imbalance.

A VIQ>PIQ profile is a good predictor of prosocial behavior. Barnett, et al. (1989) found that only 0.9% of prison inmates had such a profile compared to the 18% of the general male population, a large 20-fold difference. But what is it about a PIQ>VIQ profile that makes those evidencing this pattern more crime-prone? It may be the case that PIQ>VIQ individuals have better motor skills, given that PIQ measures assess visuospatial abilities, and it appears that they do. Yu et al. (2018) found that: "Children with discrepantly higher PIQ greater than 1SD performed significantly better on fine motor skills, compared to children with even IQD [i.e., VIQ = PIQ; the "D" = "difference"] and children with discrepantly higher VIQ greater than 1SD. Children with discrepantly higher VIQ performed significantly worse on fine motor skills than did children with discrepantly higher PIQ" (pp. 602-603). Margolis et al. (2018) investigated this in terms of cortical thickness and concluded:

> The neural system we identified seems to operate like a CT [cortical thickness] rheostat [a system that maintains or suppresses repetitive neural firing] that either improves or degrades performance of one domain-specific ability relative to the other as CT deviates either upwards or downwards from the population mean: when the cortical mantle is thin in an individual relative to the average CT of the population sample, VIQ is higher than PIQ; when the cortical mantle is thick, PIQ is higher than VIQ. ... CT has an intermediate value near the population average" (p. 14143).

Recall Shaw et al.'s (2006) 10-year longitudinal study discussed in chapter three that showed high IQ children had neural cortices that thinned more quickly than lower IQ children.

It is thus more likely the lower VIQ of most offenders rather than their superior PIQ relative to their VIQ that is salient to their offending. VIQ is more g-loaded than PIQ (Pietschnig et al. 2022) and is more important in navigating the nuances of social life. However, it is certainly not the case that a high PIQ makes a person crime-prone. Offenders only had higher PIQ *relative* to their VIQ but were still below the population average on both subscales. PIQ is enormously important to such disciplines as physics and math. One study of the mathematically gifted showed such people to have an average PIQ score of 125 and a VIQ score of 138 (Kennedy, Willcutt, & Smith, 1963).

Factors Mediating the IQ/Crime-Delinquency Relationship

The relationship between IQ and criminality has always been contentious. Adler, Mueller, and Laufer (2001, p. 109) voice the familiar criticism that IQ tests are culturally biased, despite the findings of the APA Task Force on Intelligence and subsequent work cited in chapter two. Adler, Mueller, and Laufer also cite the "debate" over whether genetics or the environment "determines" intelligence. This implies an either/or answer is possible, but since scientists involved in the study of intelligence are unanimous that all traits are *necessarily* the result of both genes and environment, it is a monumental non-debate (Flynn, 2007). Others argue that the IQ-crime relationship disappears once the effects of school performance, SES, poverty, and so on are considered.

The most usual explanation for the IQ/delinquency link is that it works via poor school performance, which leads to dropping out of school and then associating with delinquent peers (Ward & Tittle, 1994). It is thus poor school performance that allegedly makes the IQ-crime relationship disappear, with the implication that IQ is spurious. The idea that IQ influences offending via its influences on school performance was supported in 89% of 158 studies based on official statistics and 77.7% based on self-reports (Ellis & Walsh, 2000). On the other hand, all 46 studies exploring the link between grade point average (GPA) and antisocial behavior are all statistically significant in the predicted direction. Actual performance measures of academic achievements, such as GPA, are probably better predictors of antisocial behavior than IQ. Academic achievement is a measure of IQ plus many other personal and situational characteristics such as conscientious study habits, ambition, and supportive parents: talent + effort + encouragement, but we should not forget that IQ predicts so many of these things.

Children with low IQ, particularly low verbal IQ, unfortunately, lack the abilities needed for a rewarding and successful school experience. A low level of attachment and commitment to the school is an important pathway to crime in Gottfredson and Hirschi's (1990) general theory of crime. Unrewarding school experiences lead to frustration and failure and contribute to delinquency by creating non-attachment and negative attitudes toward authority figures and induce children to seek rewards in less socially desirable settings, such as among delinquent peers that provide them a sense of belonging, a set of alternate values, and a source of self-esteem. Another explanation is that children with low verbal IQ fail to fully develop higher-order social skills such as empathy and moral reasoning. In a meta-analysis of 50 studies of moral reasoning and delinquency, Stams et al. (2006) found that low levels of moral reasoning were associated with higher levels of delinquency, especially for adolescents with low IQ. Stams et al. conclude (2006): "The conclusion is that moral judgment is strongly associated with juvenile delinquency, even after controlling for socioeconomic status, culture, gender, age, and intelligence" (p. 708).

Another crucial variable mediating the IQ/crime relationship is out-of-wedlock births. In chapter six, we saw that 52% of mothers with IQs of 87 and below have children out of wedlock compared to only 3% at the top 20% with scores of 113 and above (that is over 17 times more likely), and in Murray's (2002) utopian and control samples previously discussed, the percentage of women who had given birth out-of-wedlock were: "very bright," 4%, "bright," 9%, "dull." 37%, and "very dull" 62%. Out-of-wedlock birth plays a huge role in perpetuating inter-generational poverty and crime. Using the Picture Vocabulary Test (PVT), a shortened version of the Peabody Picture Vocabulary Test-Revised that measures verbal skills and receptive vocabulary and which correlates highly with full-length Weschler IQ test scores, Beaver and Wright (2011) found that counties in the United States with the highest rates of female-headed households had the lowest IQ scores (r = - 0.56) and the highest violent crime rates (r = -0.58).

The Census Bureau (McKinnon, 2003) tells us that in 2002, only 18.8% of Black married families had an income of $25.000 ($41,246 in 2022 dollars) or less, whereas 41.1% of unmarried White female-headed families had incomes at that level. Thus, White unmarried families were more than twice as likely than Black married families to be poor. This constitutes powerful evidence against the charge that racism accounts for Black poverty and for the notion that irresponsible childbearing as its cause. McLaughlin and Mackey (2008) looked at the relationship between non-marital births and violent crime in all 50 states plus the District of Columbia from 1980 to 2004 and found that non-marital birth rates explained 48.7% of the variance in violent crime. For a generation lag of 20 years, the mean explained variance was 65.1%. Another study finds that: "Taking the U.S. as a unit, from 1951 to 2003 (or 53 years or n = 53), the correlation between out-of-wedlock births and rates of violent crime was significant. ... Over 75% ($.876^2$ = .767 = 76.7%) of the variability in rates of violent crime can be explained by differential rates of out-of-wedlock births" (Mackey & Immerman, 2007, p. 128).

A study of 240 rural counties in the United States identified high rates of female-headed households as the most important factor in explaining crime rates: "A 10 percent increase in female-headed households was associated with a 73- to 100-percent higher rates of arrest for all offenses except homicide [a 10% increase in female-headed households was associated with a 33% increase in homicide]" (Osgood & Chambers, 2003, p. 6). The problem is not just an American one. Looking at crime rates in 16 advanced countries over two centuries (from 1810 to 2010), Errol, Madsen, and Moslehi (2021, p. 535) conclude: "Our results suggest that family structure, measured by divorce rates and out-of-wedlock births, is a significantly positive determinant of violent crime, property crime, assaults, homicide and robbery over the past two centuries." African American activists Cosby and Poussaint point out: "A house without a father is a challenge. A neighborhood without fathers is a catastrophe." (2007, p. 3). Edward Kruk paints a grim picture of how catastrophic it is growing up in a fatherless home that supports this notion:

> Eighty-five percent of youth in prison have an absent father, 71% of high school dropouts are fatherless, 90% of homeless and runaway children have an absent father, and fatherless children and youth exhibit higher levels of depression and suicide, delinquency, promiscuity and teen pregnancy, behavioral problems and illicit and licit substance abuse, diminished self-concepts, and are more likely to be victims of exploitation and abuse (2012, p. 49).

Thus, all variables that allegedly render IQ spurious are intervening variables between cause and effect, and IQ undergirds them all. We have seen that IQ predicts these intervening variables and many others. IQ is an attribute that comes temporally before these variables that supposedly renders it weak or spurious is established in early childhood and is remarkably stable across the life course. For instance, the high correlation between IQ and school achievement has been found to range between 0.53 to 0.93 in a variety of studies (Sternberg, Grigorenko, & Bundy, 2001), and we have seen how well it predicts the correlated panoply of life outcomes that themselves predict crime. In other words, these other factors mediate the role of IQ on offending behavior because IQ is chronologically prior to them. Adjusting an association between IQ and criminal behavior for things such as SAT scores and SES over-adjusts and weeds out much of the very influence of IQ that we are trying to detect. To say that temporally later variables render IQ that is both prior to them and predict them makes the prior variable spurious is rather like saying that the scrambled eggs on my plate have no relationship to heat. The effects of IQ on any outcome are seldom, if ever, direct. IQ is a distal variable that leads to variables X, Y, and Z, which are the more proximate causes of crime, just like heat must combine with a frying pan, butter, and eggs, mediated by my wife's gentle hand, to make my breakfast.

The Differential Detection Hypothesis

Another objection to the IQ/crime relationship is that only the less intelligent offenders are likely to be caught and arrested. This must be true at least occasionally because disrespectful, belligerent, and impulsive offenders are more likely to get arrested, but this would be true only for minor offenses for which police have discretion as to arrest decisions. For more serious crimes for which they do not have discretion, arrest is assured regardless of an offender's attitude. Herrnstein and Murray (1994) admit that the differential detection hypothesis has intuitive appeal, but they failed to find support for it. They state that given the millions of offenders who pass through the system and whose IQs are known, "there is barely enough crime left unaccounted for to permit such a population's [a population of above-average IQ offenders] existence" (p. 243). This is not to say, of course, that above-average intelligence offenders do not exist.

Moffitt and Silva (1988) designed an elegant test of the differential detection hypothesis based on a large birth cohort of New Zealand males. Subjects were asked to self-report delinquent activity, which was then compared with official police records. This resulted in three distinct groups: (1) self-reported delinquents with a police record, (2) self-reported delinquents with no police record, and (3) nondelinquents as assessed both by self-reports and police records. Comparing IQ scores among the groups, Moffitt and Silva found that the FSIQ, VIQ, and PIQ means of groups 1 and 2 did not significantly differ from one another, meaning that undetected delinquents were no brighter than their less fortunate peers who were. Both groups had significantly lower full-scale and VIQ means, but not lower PIQ means, than nondelinquents. The nature of the sample (a large birth cohort) and the ability to match self-reports with official records make these findings compelling.

On the other hand, Yun, and Lee (2013) found that low IQ offenders were more likely to get arrested, but only in "adequate neighborhoods" and not in "disadvantaged neighborhoods," although one would intuitively expect the exact opposite. However, this study was based on self-reports only, and thus the truth of respondents' answers could not be ascertained by consulting police records. Additionally, the sample was school-based and thus missed low IQ youths who may have been absent or may have dropped out, or expelled. It would take more replication studies following the Moffitt/Silva verification model to gain more confidence in this matter, but police records of individual offenders are not available to researchers in the U.S.

Offending Among High-IQ People

Just as a high IQ does not necessarily make one wise, it does not necessarily make one moral. As Albert Einstein said: "We should take care not to make the intellect our god; it has, of course, powerful muscles, but no personality" (in Lagerfeld, 2004, p. 34). IQ has been shown to predict success in almost every domain of life, from good marriages to prestigious careers, so if a high IQ person chooses to follow an illegitimate path in life, it should predict success in that endeavor also if paired with a crime-prone personality. If a person is callous, bold, and lacks empathy, a high IQ would make him or her more successful in manipulating and victimizing others. Highly intelligent white-collar criminals, for instance, cost the economy billions of dollars and lead to bankruptcy and sometimes the suicide of their victims. Political tyrants are also men of high intelligence coupled with a lack of moral compass. The mean Weschler IQ for all Nazi war criminals tested was 127. Albert Speer had an IQ of 128, Hermann Goering 138, and although we do not have Adolf Hitler's IQ, there is little doubt that he was, as often described, an "evil genius" and a master of psychological manipulation (Zillmer, Archer, & Castino, 1989).

Serial killers are often described as having very high levels of intelligence for two reasons. The first is probably because of the high IQs of particularly notorious killers such as Ted Kaczynski (IQ = 167), Ted Bundy (IQ = 124), and Ed Kemper (IQ = 135). The second reason is that they are very difficult the catch, thus giving the impression that they are unusually smart. However, the *Radford/FGCU Annual Report on Serial Killer Statistics*, a large database of 5,334 serial killers as of 2020, finds that the average IQ of tested serial killers is 92.5 with a median of 85, which is more indicative of ordinary criminals than of the general population (Aamodt, Leary, & Southard, 2020). The IQ of the most prolific serial killer in American history, Samuel Little, who confessed to killing 93 (most of them verified), had an IQ of 96, just under the population average (Hannan, 2020). The reason that serial killers are hard to catch is not because the vast majority are too smart to get caught but because they typically target strangers, making the solving of a case particularly challenging for the police.

The evidence on offending among high IQ people is extremely sparse, and if such people are criminals, it is probably more a function of some personality deficit rather than high intelligence per se. Johansson and Kerr (2005) examined a sample of 370 incarcerated Swedish men sentenced for attempted murder, murder, or manslaughter on psychopathy and intelligence. Psychopathic and non-psychopathic criminals did not differ in intelligence, but they differed in how high intelligence was related to the seriousness of misbehavior. Among non-psychopaths, those with higher intelligence had a later start in violent crime. Among psychopaths, however, high intelligence had an early start in violent offending and more problematic behavior both inside and outside of prison walls.

To investigate the high IQ-criminality relationship, Oleson and Chappell (2012) collected self-report questionnaires from a high-IQ sample of individuals from a high-IQ society requiring a 99.9 percentile IQ score to belong and from students from elite US and UK universities to act as a control group. The average IQ of the high-IQ sample (n = 465) was 154.6, and the average IQ for the control sample (n = 756) was estimated to be 100. The high-IQ sample reported a mean of 13.9 offenses, and the control sample reported a mean of 9.6 offenses. The high-IQ sample also reported a higher rate of attempted suicide (13.1%) versus 8.3 % in the control group. Oleson and Chappell (2012, p. 725) concluded: "To summarize, the high-IQ sample reported higher prevalence rates than the control group for six of the eight measured offenses. The opposite was true only for threats and assault. The difference between prevalence rates was statistically significant for homicide [4 subjects in the high-IQ category admitted to this], bomb-making, and aggregated violent offending. Incidence rates were greater for high-IQ subjects than for controls for all offenses except robbery." It seems that antisocial offending dips and rises according to IQ. It is low among the 2.2% of the population of individuals who are relatively incapable of offending (IQ < 70), rises slowly and then precipitously among those with IQs between 80 to 95, dips among those with IQs in the average to superior range (100 to 129), and then rises a little among the 2.2% of the population who are a very superior group (IQ > 130).

Thus, we are all capable of committing crimes regardless of our IQ, but an average and above IQ is a protective factor. But such an IQ is only a Kevlar vest that covers only vital areas and not something that covers all risks. As in all areas of life, a high IQ can make a person more successful in a life of crime if he or she possesses a personality profile that may lead him or her to choose such a lifestyle. If the potential rewards are sufficiently great and the risk of detection is sufficiently low, most of us may cross the criminality threshold.

References

Aamodt, M., Leary, T., & Southard, L. (2020). *Radford/FGCU Annual Report on Serial Killer Statistics: 2020.* Radford, VA: Radford University.

Adkins, D., & Guo, G. (2008). Societal development and the shifting influence of the genome on status attainment. *Research in Social Stratification and Mobility, 26:* 235-255.

Adler, F., Mueller, G., & Laufer, W. (2001). Criminology and the justice system. New York: McGraw-Hill.

Adolphs, R. (2009). The social brain: Neural basis of social knowledge. *Annual Review of Psychology,* 60: 693-716.

Anderson, M. (2008). Multiple inference and gender differences in the effects of early intervention: A reevaluation of the Abecedarian, Perry Preschool, and Early Training Projects. *Journal of the American statistical Association, 103:* 1481-1495.

Anglim, J., Dunlop, P., Wee, S., Horwood, S., Wood, J., & Marty, A. (2022). Personality and intelligence: A meta-analysis. *Psychological Bulletin, 148:* 301-336.

Arce-Ferrer, A., & Martinez Guzman, E. (2009). Studying the equivalence of computer-delivered and paper-based administrations of the raven standard progressive matrices test. *Educational and psychological measurement, 69:* 855-867.

Ash, J., & Gallup, G. (2007). Paleoclimatic variation and brain expansion during human evolution. *Human Nature, 18:* 109-124.

Bailey, D. & Geary, D. (2009). Hominid brain evolution: Testing climactic, ecological, and social competition models. *Human Nature,* 20:67-79.

Baker, L., Bezdjian, S., & Raine, A. (2006). Behavioral genetics: The science of antisocial behavior. *Law and contemporary problems, 69:* 7-46.

Barnett, R., Zimmer, L., & McCormack, J. (1989). P>V sign and personality profiles. *Journal of Correctional and Social Psychiatry,* 35: 18-20.

Basmajian, J. (1985). Keynote address: The next clinical revolution-behavioral medicine. *The Journal of the American Osteopathic Association, 85*(9), 84-86.

Bates, T. & Gignac, G. (2022). Effort impacts IQ test scores in a minor way: A multi-study investigation with healthy adult volunteers. *Intelligence, 92:* 101652.

Beaver, K., & Wright, J. (2011). The association between county-level IQ and county-level crime rates. *Intelligence, 39:* 22-26.

Bellinger, D. (2008). Neurological and behavioral consequences of childhood lead exposure. *PLoS Medicine,* 5: 690–692.

Betjemann, R., Johnson, E., Barnard, H., Boada, R., Filley, C., Filipek, P., Willcutt, E. DeFries, J., & Pennington, B. (2010). Genetic covariation between brain volumes and IQ, reading performance, and processing speed. *Behavior Genetics, 40:* 135-145.

Bird, K. (2021). No support for the hereditarian hypothesis of the Black–White achievement gap using polygenic scores and tests for divergent selection. *American Journal of Physical Anthropology, 175:* 465-476.

Bond, R. & Saunders, P. (1999). Routes of Success: Influences on the occupational attainment of young British males. *British Journal of Sociology,* 50: 217-240.

Bouchard Jr, T. (1998). Genetic and environmental influences on adult intelligence and special mental abilities. *Human biology,* 257-279.

Bouchard Jr, T. & McGue, M. (1981). Familial studies of intelligence: A review. *Science, 212:* 1055-1059.

Bouchard Jr, T. & McGue, M. (2003). Genetic and environmental influences on human psychological differences. *Journal of Neurobiology,* 54: 4-45.

Bouchard Jr, T., & Segal, N. (1985). Environment and IQ. *Handbook of intelligence: Theories, measurements, and applications,* 391-464.

Boyce, W., & Kobor, M. (2015). Development and the epigenome: the 'synapse' of gene–environment interplay. *Developmental science, 18:* 1-23.

Brass, M., & Cramon, D. (2004). Decomposing components of task preparation with functional magnetic resonance imaging. *Journal of cognitive neuroscience, 16:* 609-620.

Bratsberg, B., & Rogeberg, O. (2018). Flynn effect and its reversal are both environmentally caused. *Proceedings of the National Academy of Sciences,* 115(: 6674-6678.

Burt, C., & Simons, R. (2015). Heritability studies in the postgenomic era: The fatal flaw is conceptual. *Criminology, 53:* 103-112.

Buschkuehl, M. & Jaeggi, S. (2010). Improving intelligence: A literature review. *Swiss Medical Weekly,* 140:266-272.

Cai, B., Zhang, G., Zhang, A., Xiao, L., Hu, W., Stephen, J., Wilson, T., Calhoun, V., & Wang, Y. (2021). Functional connectome fingerprinting: identifying individuals and predicting cognitive functions via autoencoder. *Human Brain Mapping, 42:* 2691-2705.

Calvin, C., Deary, I., Fenton, C., Roberts, B., Der, G., Leckenby, N., & Batty, G. (2011). Intelligence in youth and all-cause-mortality: systematic review with meta-analysis. *International journal of epidemiology, 40:* 626-644.

Carey, G. (2003). *Human genetics for the social sciences.* Thousand Oaks, CA: Sage.

Carey, N. (2012). *The epigenetics revolution: How modern biology is rewriting our understanding of genetics, disease, and inheritance.* New York: Columbia University Press.

Casey, B., Somerville, L., Gotlib, I., Ayduk, O., Franklin, N., Askrend, M., Jonides, J., Berman, M., Wilson, M., Teslovich, T., Glover, G. (2011). Behavioral and neural correlates of delay of gratification 40 years later. *Proceedings of the National Academy of Sciences,* 108: 14998-15004.

Caspi, A., Bem, D., & Elder, G. (1989). Continuities and consequences of interaction styles across the lifecourse. *Journal of Personality,* 57:375-406.

Caspi, A., Williams, B., Kim-Cohen, J., Craig, I., Milne, B., Poulton, R., ... & Moffitt, T. (2007). Moderation of breastfeeding effects on the IQ by genetic variation in fatty acid metabolism. *Proceedings of the National Academy of Sciences, 104:*18860-18865.

Casswell, S., Pledger, M., & Hooper, R. (2003). Socioeconomic status and drinking patterns in young adults. *Addiction, 98:* 601-610.

Ceci, S., & Williams, W. (2009). Should scientists study race and IQ? YES: The scientific truth must be pursued. Nature, 457: 788–789.

Cecil, K., Brubaker, C., Adler, C., Dietrich, K., Altaye, M., Egelhoff, J., ... Lanphear, B. (2008). Decreased brain volume in adults with childhood lead exposure. *PLoS Medicine,* 5: 742–750.

Center for Disease Control (2002). Fetal alcohol syndrome—Alaska, Arizona, Colorado, and New York. 1995–1997. http://www.cdc.gov/mmwr/preview/mmwrhtml/mm5120a2.htm.

Chabris, C., Lee, J., Cesarini, D., Benjamin, D., & Laibson, D. (2015). The fourth law of behavior genetics. *Current Directions in Psychological Science, 24:* 304-312.

Chakraborty, B., Lee, H., Wolujewicz, M., Mallik, J., Sun, G., Dietrich, K., & Chakraborty, R. (2008). Low dose effect of chronic lead exposure on neuromotor response impairment in children is moderated by genetic polymorphisms. *Journal of Human Ecology,* 23: 183–194.

Chamorro-Premuzic, T. & Furman, A. (2005). intellectual competence. *The Psychologist,* 18: 352-354.

Charlton, B. (2009). Clever sillies: Why high IQ people tend to be deficient in common sense. *Medical Hypotheses,* 73: 867-870.

Child Trends Data Bank (2013). Child maltreatment. http://www.childtrends.org/?indicators=child-maltreatment.

Child Trends Data Bank (2014). Infant homicides. http://www.childtrends.org/?indicators=infant-homicide.

Ciotti, P. (1998). Money and school performance: Lessons from the Kansas City desegregation experiment. *Policy Analysis, 298:* 1-25.

Clark, C., & Gist, N. (1938). Intelligence as a factor in occupational choice. *American Sociological Review, 3:* 683-694.

Cloward, R. & Ohlin, L. (1960). *Delinquency and opportunity.* New York: Free Press.

Cofnas, N. (2020). Research on group differences in intelligence: A defense of free inquiry. *Philosophical Psychology, 33:* 125-147.

Cohen, A. (1955). *Delinquent boys.* New York: Free Press.

Cosby, B & Poussaint, A. (2007). *Come on, people: On the path from victims to victors.* Nashville, Thomas Nelson.

Cozolino, L. (2014). *The neuroscience of human relationships: Attachment and the developing social brain (Norton Series on Interpersonal Neurobiology).* WW Norton & Company.

Crozier, J., & Barth, R. (2005). Cognitive and academic functioning in maltreated children. *Children & Schools, 27:* 197-206.

Deary, I. (2003). Reaction time and psychometric intelligence: Jensen's contributions. In Nyborg, H. (ed.). *The scientific study of general intelligence: Tribute to Arthur Jensen,* pp. 53-75. Elsevier.

Deary, I., Cox, S., & Hill, W. (2022). Genetic variation, brain, and intelligence differences. *Molecular psychiatry, 27*(1), 335-353.

Deary, I., Johnson, W., & Houlihan, L. (2009). Genetic foundations of human intelligence. *Human genetics, 126:* 215-232.

Deary, I., Penke, L., & Johnson, W. (2010). The neuroscience of human intelligence differences. *Nature reviews neuroscience, 11:* 201-211.

Deary, I., Spinath, F., & Bates, T. (2006). Genetics of intelligence. *European Journal of Human Genetics, 14:* 690-700.

Deary, I., Whalley, L., Lemmon, H., Crawford, J., & Starr, J. (2000). The stability of individual differences in mental ability from childhood to old age: Follow-up of the 1932 Scottish Mental Survey. *Intelligence, 28:* 49-55.

Deary, I., Weiss, A., & Batty, G. D. (2010). Intelligence and personality as predictors of illness and death: How researchers in differential psychology and chronic disease epidemiology are collaborating to understand and address health inequalities. *Psychological Science in the Public Interest, 11:* 53-79.

Deming, D. (2017). The growing importance of social skills in the labor market. *Quarterly Journal of Economics,* 132: 1593–640.

Department of Health and Human Services (2004). Breastfeeding practices—Results from the National Immunization Survey. http://www.cdc.gov/breastfeeding/data/NIS_2004.htm.

Depue, R., & Collins, P. (1999). Neurobiology of the structure of personality: Dopamine, facilitation of incentive motivation, and extraversion. *Behavioral and Brain Sciences, 22:* 491-517.

DeWeerdt, S. (2019). How to map the Brain. *Nature.* Doi: 10.1038/d41586-019-02208-0.

Dickens, W. & Flynn, J. (2001). Heritability estimates versus large environmental effects; The IQ paradox resolved. *Psychological Review,* 108: 346-349.

DiRago, A., & Vaillant, G. (2007). Resilience in inner city youth: Childhood predictors of occupational status across the lifespan. *Journal of Youth and Adolescence, 36:* 61-70.

Dizaji, A., Vieira, B., Khodaei, M., Ashrafi, M., Parham, E., Hosseinzadeh, G., Salmon, C. & Soltanianzadeh, H., 2021. Linking brain biology to intellectual endowment: A review on the associations of human intelligence with neuroimaging data. *Basic and Clinical Neuroscience, 12:* 1-27.

Dobson, K., Chow, C., Morrison, K., & Van Lieshout, R. (2017). Associations between childhood cognition and cardiovascular events in adulthood: a systematic review and meta-analysis. *Canadian Journal of Cardiology, 33:* 232-242.

Dugdale, R. (1877/1895). *"The Jukes": A study in crime, pauperism, disease, and heredity.* New York: Putnam.

Duckworth, A., Quinn, P., Lynam, D., Loeber, R., & Stouthamer-Loeber, M. (2011). Role of test motivation in intelligence testing. *Proceedings of the National Academy of Sciences, 108:* 7716-7720.

Durkheim, E. (1951). The division *of labor in society.* Glencoe, IL: Free Press.

Dutton, E., & van der Linden, D. (2015). Who are the "Clever Sillies"? The intelligence, personality, and motives of clever silly originators and those who follow them. *Intelligence, 49:* 57-65.

Edelman, G. (1992). *Bright air, brilliant fire.* New York: Basic Books.

Edwards, A. (2003). Human genetic diversity: Lewontin's fallacy. *BioEssays,* 25:798-801.

Ehrlich, D. E., & Josselyn, S. A. (2016). Plasticity-related genes in brain development and amygdala-dependent learning. *Genes, Brain and Behavior, 15:* 125-143.

Ellis, B. (1995). The evolution of sexual attraction: Evaluative mechanisms in women. In Barkow, J., Cosmides, L. & Tooby, J. (eds.), *The adapted mind: evolutionary psychology and the generation of culture,* pp. 267-288. New York: Oxford University Press.

Ellis, L. (1996). A discipline in peril: Sociology's future hinges on curing its biophobia. *The American Sociologist, 27:* 21-41.

Ellis, L. & Walsh, A. (2000). *Criminology: A global perspective.* Boston: Allyn & Bacon.

Ellis, L., & Walsh, A. (2003). Crime, delinquency, and intelligence: A review of the worldwide literature. In H. Nyborg (Ed.), *The Scientific Study of General Intelligence: Tribute to Arthur J. Jensen,* pp. 343–365. Kidlington, Oxford: Elsevier Science.

Eppig, C., Fincher, C., & Thornhill, R. (2010). Parasite prevalence and the worldwide distribution of cognitive ability. *Proceedings of the Royal Society B: Biological Sciences, 277:* 3801-3808.

Eppig, C., Fincher, C., & Thornhill, R. (2011). Parasite prevalence and the distribution of intelligence among the states of the USA. *Intelligence, 39:* 155-160.

Errol, Z., Madsen, J., & Moslehi, S. (2021). Social disorganization theory and crime in the advanced countries: Two centuries of evidence. *Journal of Economic Behavior & Organization, 191:* 519-537.

Farrington, D. & Welsh, B. (2007). Saving children from a life of crime: Early risk factors and effective interventions. New York, NY: Oxford University Press.

Felson, J. (2014). What can we learn from twin studies? A comprehensive evaluation of the qual environments assumption. *Social Science Research,* 43:184–199.

Figueredo, A., Vásquez, G., Brumbach, B.., Schneider, S., Sefcek, J., Tal, I., Hill, D., Wenner, C., & Jacobs, W., (2006). Consilience and life history theory: From genes to brain to reproductive strategy. *Developmental Review, 26:* 243-275.

Fincher, J. (1982). *The human brain: Mystery of matter and mind.* Washington, DC: U.S. News Books.

Finn, E., Shen, X., Scheinost, D., Rosenberg, M., Huang, J., Chun, M., Papademetris, X., & Constable, R. (2015). Functional connectome fingerprinting: identifying individuals using patterns of brain connectivity. *Nature neuroscience, 18:* 1664-1671.

Flynn, J. (2007). *What is intelligence? Beyond the Flynn effect.* Cambridge: Cambridge University Press.

Flynn, J. (2013). The "Flynn effect" and Flynn's paradox. *Intelligence, 41:* 851-857.

Forero, D., Pereira-Morales, A., & González-Giraldo, Y. (2017). Molecular genetics and human behavior. *Module in Neuroscience and Biobehavioral Psychology.* http://dx.doi.org/10.1016/B978-0-12-809324-5.06489-0

Frisell, T., Pawitan, Y., & Långström, N. (2012). Is the association between general cognitive ability and violent crime caused by family-level confounders? *PloS one, 7:* e41783.

Gabora, L., & Russon, A. (2011). The evolution of human intelligence. In R. Sternberg & S. Kaufman (eds.), The Cambridge handbook of intelligence, pp. 328-350. Cambridge: Cambridge University Press.

Gale, C., Batty, G., Tynelius, P., Deary, I., & Rasmussen, F. (2010). Intelligence in early adulthood and subsequent hospitalisation and admission rates for the whole range of mental disorders: longitudinal study of 1,049,663 men. *Epidemiology (Cambridge, Mass.), 21:* 70-77.

Gardner, H. (2001). The ethical responsibilities of professionals. http://thegoodproject.org/wp-content/uploads/2012/09/GoodWork2.pdf

Garlick, D. (2002). Understanding the nature of the general factor of intelligence: the role of individual differences in neural plasticity as an explanatory mechanism. *Psychological review, 109:* 116-136.

Garlick, D. (2003). Integrating brain science research with intelligence research. *Current Directions in Psychological Science, 12:* 185-189.

Gatzke-Kopp, L, Raine, A., Loeber, R., Stouthamer-Loeber, M., & Steinhauer, S. (2002). Serious delinquent behavior, sensation seeking, and electrodermal arousal. *Journal of Abnormal Child Psychology,* 30:477-486.

Geary, D. C. (2005). *The origin of mind: Evolution of brain, cognition, and general intelligence.* Washington, DC: American Psychological Association.

Gewertz, C. (2000). A hard lesson for Kansas City's troubled schools. *Education Week,* April 22, 1-5.

Giedd, J. (2004). Structural magnetic resonance imaging of the adolescent brain. *Annals of the New York Academy of Sciences, 1021:* 77-85.

Gigi, K., Werbeloff, N., Goldberg, S., Portuguese, S., Reichenberg, A., Fruchter, E., & Weiser, M. (2014). Borderline intellectual functioning is associated with poor social functioning, increased rates of psychiatric diagnosis and drug use–A cross sectional population based study. *European Neuropsycho pharmacology, 24:* 1793-1797.

Glahn, D., Thompson, P., & Blangero, J. (2007). Neuroimaging endophenotypes: strategies for finding genes influencing brain structure and function. *Human brain mapping, 28:* 488-501.

Glueck S, & Glueck E (1950) *Unraveling juvenile delinquency.* New York: Commonwealth Fund.

Goddard, H. (1912/1931). *The Kallikak family: A study in the heredity of feeble-mindedness.* New York: Macmillan.

Goddard, H. (1914). *Feeblemindedness: Its causes and consequences.* New York: Macmillan.

Gordon, R. (1997). Everyday life as an intelligence test: Effects of intelligence and intelligence context. *Intelligence, 24:* 203-320.

Gottfredson, L. (1986). Societal consequences of the g factor in employment. *Journal of Vocational Behavior, 29:* 379-410.

Gottfredson, L. (1997). Why g matters: The complexity of everyday life. *Intelligence, 24:* 79-132.

Gottfredson, L. (2004). Intelligence: Is it the epidemiologists' elusive "fundamental cause" of social class inequalities in health? *Journal of Personality and Social Psychology, 86:* 174-199.

Gottfredson, L. (2005). What if the hereditarian hypothesis is true? *Psychology, Public Policy, and Law,* 11: 311-319.

Gottfredson, M. & Hirschi, T. (1990). *A general theory of crime.* Stanford: Stanford University Press.

Gray, J., & Thompson, P. (2004). Neurobiology of intelligence: science and ethics. *Nature Reviews Neuroscience, 5:* 471-482.

Gunnar, M., & Quevedo, K. (2007). The neurobiology of stress and development. *Annual Review of Psychology, 58:* 145-173.

Gur, R., Butler, E., Moore, T., Rosen, A., Ruparel, K., Satterthwaite, T., Roalf, D., Gennatas, E., Bilker, W., Shinohara, R., & Port, A. (2020). Structural and functional brain parameters related to cognitive performance across development: Replication and extension of the Parieto-Frontal Integration Theory in a single sample, *Cerebral Cortex,* 00: 1–20.

Hacking, I. (2006). Genetics, biosocial groups & the future of identity. *Daedalus,* 135: 81–95.

Hannan, S. (2020). The crimes of America's most prolific serial killer. *The Cleveland Magazine,* January. https://clevelandmagazine.com/in-the-cle/the-read/articles/in-the-shadows.

Hart, C., Taylor, M., Smith, G., Whalley, L., Starr, J., Hole, D., Wilson, V. and Deary, I. (2004). Childhood IQ and cardiovascular disease in adulthood: prospective observational study linking the Scottish Mental Survey 1932 and the Midspan studies. *Social Science & Medicine, 59:* 2131-2138.

Hatemi, P., McDermott, R., & Eaves, L. (2015). Genetic and environmental contributions to relationships and divorce attitudes. *Personality and individual differences, 72:* 135-140.

Hayes, T., Petrov, A., & Sederberg, P. (2015). Do we really become smarter when our fluid-intelligence test scores improve? *Intelligence, 48,* 1-14.

Hecht, E. (2007). Energy and change. *The Physics Teacher, 45:* 88-92.

Heck, K., Braveman, P., Cubbin, C., Chávez, G., & Kiely, J. (2006). Socioeconomic status and breastfeeding initiation among California mothers. *Public health reports, 121:* 51-59.

Herrnstein, R.., & Murray, C. (1994). *The bell curve: Intelligence and class structure in American life.* New York: Free Press.

Hill, W., Davies, G., McIntosh, A., Gale, C., & Deary, I. (2017). A combined analysis of genetically correlated traits identifies 107 loci associated with intelligence. *BioRxiv,* 160291.

Hill W., Marioni R., Maghzian O, Ritchie S., Hagenaars S., McIntosh A., Gale C., Davies G., & Deary I. (2019). A combined analysis of genetically correlated traits identifies 187 loci and a role for neurogenesis and myelination in intelligence. *Molecular Psychiatry* 24: 169–181.

Isen, J. (2010). A meta-analytic assessment of Wechsler's P>V sign in antisocial populations. *Clinical psychology review, 30:* 423-435.

Jackson, K., & Nazar, A. (2006). Breastfeeding, the immune response, and long-term health. *Journal of Osteopathic Medicine, 106:* 203-207.

Jacob, L., Haro, J., & Koyanagi, A. (2019). Association between intelligence quotient and violence perpetration in the English general population. *Psychological medicine, 49:* 1316-1323.

Jensen, A. (1998). *The g factor.* Westport, CT: Praeger.

Jensen, A., & Figueroa, R. (1975). Forward and backward digit span interaction with race and IQ: predictions from Jensen's theory. *Journal of Educational Psychology, 67:* 882-893.

Jin, W., Yang, K., Barzilay, R., & Jaakkola, T. (2018). Learning multimodal graph-to-graph translation for molecular optimization. *arXiv preprint arXiv: 1812.01070.*

Johansson, P., & Kerr, M. (2005). Psychopathy and intelligence: A second look. *Journal of personality disorders, 19:* 357-369.

Johnson, A., Lee, J. & Leeuw, C. (2014). Common genetic variants associated with cognitive performance identified using the proxy-phenotype method. *Proceedings of the National Academy of Sciences, 111:* 13790-13794.

Joo, Y., Cha, J., Freese, J., & Hayes, M. (2022). Cognitive capacity Genome-Wide Polygenic Scores identify individuals with slower cognitive decline in aging. *Genes, 13:* 1320.

Jung, R., & Haier, R. (2007). The Parieto-Frontal Integration Theory (P-FIT) of intelligence: converging neuroimaging evidence. *Behavioral and brain sciences, 30:* 135-154.

Kanazawa, S. (2008). Temperature and evolutionary novelty as forces behind the evolution of general intelligence. *Intelligence, 36:* 99-108.

Kanazawa, S. (2012). The evolution of general intelligence. *Personality and Individual Differences, 53:* 90-93.

Kennedy, W., Willcutt, H., & Smith, A. (1963). Wechsler profiles of mathematically gifted adolescents. *Psychological Reports, 12:* 259-262.

Keyes, K., Platt, J., Kaufman, A., & McLaughlin, K. (2017). Association of fluid intelligence and psychiatric disorders in a population-representative sample of US adolescents. *Journal of the American Medical Association: Psychiatry, 74:* 179-188.

Kingston, P. (2006). How meritocratic is the United States? *Research in Social Stratification and Mobility,* 24:11-130.

Koller, K., Brown, T., Spurfeon, A., & Levy, L. (2004). Recent developments in low-level lead exposure and intellectual impairment in children. *Environmental Health Perspectives,* 112: 987–994.

Kourany, J. (2016). Should some knowledge be forbidden? The case of cognitive differences research. *Philosophy of Science, 83:* 779-790.

Kramer, M., Aboud, F., Mironova, E., Vanilovich, I., Platt, R., Matush, L., ... Shapiro, S. (2008). Breastfeeding and child cognitive development: New evidence from a large randomized trial. *Archives of General Psychiatry,* 65: 578–584.

Kruk, E. (2012). Arguments for an equal parental responsibility presumption in contested child custody. *The American Journal of Family Therapy, 40*:33-55.

Lagerfeld, S. (2004). The revenge of the nerds. *The Wilson Quarterly (1976-), 28:* 28-34. (ADHD). *PloS one, 8*(4), e62177.

Landecker, H. & Panofsky, A. (2013). From social structure to gene regulation, and back: A critical introduction to environmental epigenetics for sociology. *Annual Review of Sociology* 39: 333-357.

Langeslag, S., Schmidt, M., Ghassabian, A., Jaddoe, V., Hofman, A., van der Lugt, A., Verhulst, F., Tiemeier, H. and White, T. (2013). Functional connectivity between parietal and frontal brain regions and intelligence in young children: the Generation R study. *Human Brain Mapping, 34:* 3299-3307.

Laundra, K., & Sutton, T. (2008). You think you know ghetto? Contemporizing the dove "Black IQ test". *Teaching sociology, 36:* 366-377.

Lechner, C. M., Miyamoto, A., & Knopf, T. (2019). Should students be smart, curious, or both? Fluid intelligence, openness, and interest co-shape the acquisition of reading and math competence. *Intelligence, 76:* 101378.

Lee J., Wedow, R., Okbay, A., Kong, E., Maghzian, O., Zacher, M., Nguyen-Viet, T., Bowers, P., Sidorenko, J., Karlsson Linner, R., Fontana, M., Kundu, T., Lee, C., Li, H., Li, R., Royer, R., Timshel, P., Walters, R., Willoughby, E., Yengo, L., et al. (2018). Gene discovery and polygenic prediction from a genome-wide association study of educational attainment in 1.1 million individuals. *Nature Genetics* 50: 1112–1121.

Lewontin, R. (1970). Race and intelligence. *Bulletin of the Atomic Scientists, 26*(3), 2-8.

Lewontin, R. (1972). The apportionment of human diversity. *Evolutionary Biology*, 6:391–398.

Lipsey, M., Farran, D., & Durkin, K. (2018). Effects of the Tennessee Prekindergarten Program on children's achievement and behavior through third grade. *Early Childhood Research Quarterly, 45:* 155-176.

Little, B., Sud, N., Nobile, Z., & Bhattacharya, D. (2021). Teratogenic effects of maternal drug abuse on developing brain and underlying neurotransmitter mechanisms. N*eurotoxicology, 86:* 172-179.

Lubinski, D. (2004). Introduction to the special section on cognitive abilities: 100 years after Spearman's (1904) "General intelligence," objectively determined and measured." *Journal of Personality and Social Psychology, 86:* 96-111.

Lykken, D. (1995). *The Antisocial Personalities*. Hillsdale, NJ: Lawrence Erlbaum.

Lynch, J., Smith, G., Harper, S., Hillemeier, M., Ross, N., Kaplan, G., & Wolfson, M. (2004). Is income inequality a determinant of population health? Part 1. A systematic review. *The Milbank Quarterly, 82:* 5-99.

Lynn, R. (2009). What has caused the Flynn effect? Secular increases in the development quotients of infants. *Intelligence*, 37:16-24.

Lynn, R., Fuerst, J., & Kirkegaard, E. (2018). Regional differences in intelligence in 22 countries and their economic, social and demographic correlates: A review. *Intelligence, 69:* 24-36.

Mackenbach, J. (2002). Income inequality and population health. *British Medical Journal*, 324: 1–2.

Mackey, W., & Immerman, R. (2007). Fatherlessness by divorce contrasted to fatherlessness by non-marital births: A distinction with a difference for the community. *Journal of Divorce & Remarriage, 47:* 111-134.

Mani, M., Kabekkodu, S., Joshi, M., & Dsouza, H. (2019). Ecogenetics of lead toxicity and its influence on risk assessment. *Human & Experimental Toxicology, 38:* 1031-1059.

Margolis, A., Bansal, R., Hao, X., Algermissen, M., Erickson, C., Klahr, K., Naglieri, J. & Peterson, B. (2018). Using IQ discrepancy scores to examine the neural correlates of specific cognitive abilities. *Journal of Neuroscience, 33:*14135-14145.

Matarazzo, J. (1976). *Wechsler's measurement and appraisal of adult intelligence.* Baltimore: Williams and Wilkins.

May, P., Gossage, J., Marais, A., Hendricks, L., Snell, C., Tabachnick, B., Stellavato, C., Buckley, D., Brooke, L., & Viljoen, D., (2008). Maternal risk factors for fetal alcohol syndrome and partial fetal alcohol syndrome in South Africa: a third study. *Alcoholism: Clinical and Experimental Research, 32:* pp.738-753.

McKinnon, J. (2003). *The Black Population in the United States:* March 2002. Washington, DC: U.S. Census Bureau.

McGloin, J., & Pratt, T. (2003). Cognitive ability and delinquent behavior among inner-city youth: A life-course analysis of main, mediating, and interaction effects. *International Journal of Offender Therapy and Comparative Criminology, 47:* 253-271.

McLaughlin, V., & Mackey, W. (2008). Demographics of the upward-trending murder rate in Buffalo, New York: A harbinger of societal stress. *Journal of Social, Political, and Economic Studies, 33:* 458-471.

Medina, H., Callahan, K., Koru-Sengul, T., Maheshwari, S., Liu, Q., Goel, N., & Pinheiro, P. (2022). Elevated breast cancer mortality among highly educated Asian American women. *Plos one, 17*(5): e0268617.

Meldrum, R., Petkovsek, M., Boutwell, B., & Young, J. (2017). Reassessing the relationship between general intelligence and self-control in childhood. *Intelligence, 60:* 1-9.

Merton, R. (1938). Social structure and anomie. *American Sociological Review* 3: 672–82.

Miller, L. (1987). Neuropsychology of the aggressive psychopath: An integrative review. *Aggressive Behavior,* 13: 119-140.

Mills, M., & Tropf, F. (2020). Sociology, genetics, and the coming of age of sociogenomics. *Annual Review of Sociology, 46*(1), 553-581.

Mitchell, C., Hobcraft, J., McLanahan, S., Siegel, S., Berg, A., Brooks-Gunn, J., & Notterman, D. (2014). Social disadvantage, genetic sensitivity, and children's telomere length. *Proceedings of the National Academy of Sciences,* 111: 5944–5949.

Mitchell, K. (2007). The genetics of brain wiring: From molecule to mind. *PLoS Biology,* 4: 690-692.

Missouri v. Jenkins, 495 U.S. 33 (1990)

Missouri v. Jenkins II, 515 U.S. 70 (1995).

Moffitt, T. (1993). Adolescent-limited and life-course-persistent antisocial behavior: A developmental taxonomy. *Psychological Review*, 100: 674-701.

Moffitt T., Arseneault, L., Belsky, D., Dickson, N., Hancox, R., Harrington, H., Hout, R., Poulton, R., Roberts, B., Ross, S., Sears, M., Thomson, W., & Caspi, A. (2011). A gradient of childhood self-control predicts health, wealth, and public safety. *Proceedings of the National Academy of Sciences*, 108: 2693-2698.

Moffitt, T., & Beckley, A. (2015). Abandon twin research? Embrace epigenetic research? Premature advice for criminologists. *Criminology*, 53: 121–126.

Moffitt, T., Gabrielli, W., Mednick, S., & Schulsinger, F. (1981). Socioeconomic status, IQ, and delinquency. *Journal of Abnormal Psychology*, 90: 152.

Moffitt, T., & Silva, P. (1988). IQ and delinquency: a direct test of the differential detection hypothesis. *Journal of abnormal psychology*, 97: 330-333.

Murray, C. (2002). IQ and income inequality in a sample of sibling pairs from advantaged family backgrounds. *The American Economic Review*, 92: 339-343.

Neisser, U., Boodoo, G., Bouchard, T., Boykin, A., Brody, N., Ceci, S., Halpern, D., Loehlin, J., Perloff, R., Sternberg, R. & Urbina, S. (1996). Intelligence: Knowns and unknowns. *American Psychologist*, 51: 77-101.

Nettle, D. (2003). Intelligence and class mobility in the British population. *British Journal of Psychology*, 94: 551-561.

Nettler, G. (1984). *Explaining crime* (3rd Ed.). New York: McGraw Hill.

Neubauer, A., & Fink, A. (2009). Intelligence and neural efficiency. *Neuroscience & Biobehavioral Reviews*, 33: 1004-1023.

Nielsen, F. (2006). Achievement and ascription in educational attainment: Genetic and environmental influences on adolescent schooling. *Social Forces*, 85: 193-216.

Nisbett, R., Aronson, J., Blair, C., Dickens, W., Flynn, J., Halpern, D., & Turkheimer, E. (2012). Intelligence: new findings and theoretical developments. *American psychologist*, 67: 130-159.

Nguyen, H., & Ryan, A. (2008). Does stereotype threat affect test performance of minorities and women? A meta-analysis of experimental evidence. *Journal of applied psychology*, 93: 1314-1334.

Nolan, B., Richiardi, M., & Valenzuela, L. (2019). The drivers of income inequality in rich countries. *Journal of Economic Surveys*, 33: 1285-1324.

O'Connell, M., Boat, T., & Warner, K.. (2009). Committee on the prevention of mental disorders and substance abuse among children, youth, and young adults: research advances and promising interventions. *Preventing mental, emotional, and behavioral disorders among young people: Progress and possibilities.* Washington, DC: The National Academies Press.

O'Connell, M., & Marks, G. (2021). Are the effects of intelligence on student achievement and well-being largely functions of family income and social class? Evidence from a longitudinal study of Irish adolescents. *Intelligence, 84*, 101511.

Oleson, J., & Chappell, R. (2012). Self-reported violent offending among subjects with genius-level IQ scores. *Journal of family violence, 27*: 715-730.

Oregon Department of Human Services (2002). Gaining knowledge about fetal alcohol syndrome. https://public.health.oregon.gov/HealthyPeopleFamilies/Women/PreconceptionHealth/FetalAlcoholSyndrome/Documents/fas_final _report.pdf.

Osgood, D. & Chambers, J. (2003). Community correlates of rural youth violence. Washington, DC: *Juvenile Justice Bulletin*, May. U.S. Department of Justice.

Penn, A. (2001). Early brain wiring: activity-dependent processes. *Schizophrenia Bulletin, 27:* 337-347.

Pesta, B., & Poznanski, P. (2014). Only in America: Cold Winters Theory, race, IQ and well-being. *Intelligence, 46:* 271-274.

Petkovsek, M., & Boutwell, B. (2014). Childhood intelligence and the emergence of self-control. *Criminal Justice and Behavior, 41:* 1232-1249.

Petty, M. (2010). The IQ myth. http://www.selfgrowth.com/articles/the-iq-myth.

Pietschnig, J., Gerdesmann, D., Zeiler, M., & Voracek, M. (2022). Of differing methods, disputed estimates and discordant interpretations: the meta-analytical multiverse of brain volume and IQ associations. *Royal Society Open Science, 9:* 211621.

Pietschnig, J., & Voracek, M. (2015). One century of global IQ gains: A formal meta-analysis of the Flynn effect (1909–2013). *Perspectives on Psychological Science, 10:* 282-306.

Piquero, A., & White, N. (2003). On the relationship between cognitive abilities and life-course-persistent offending among a sample of African Americans: A longitudinal test of Moffitt's hypothesis. *Journal of Criminal Justice, 31:* 399-409.

Pirnahad, K. (2007). *Evolution of humanity: The path to independence*. New York: iUniverse, Inc.

Plomin, R., & von Stumm, S. (2018). The new genetics of intelligence. *Nature Reviews Genetics*, 19: 148. doi: 10.1038/nrg.2017.104.

Polderman, T., Benyamin, B., De Leeuw, C., Sullivan, P., Van Bochoven, A., Visscher, P., & Posthuma, D. (2015). Meta-analysis of the heritability of human traits based on fifty years of twin studies. *Nature Genetics, 47:* 702-709.

Posthuma, D., De Geus, E., Baaré, W., Pol, H., Kahn, R., & Boomsma, D. (2002). The association between brain volume and intelligence is of genetic origin. *Nature neuroscience, 5:* 83-84.

Prayer, D., Kasprian, G., Krampl, E., Ulm, B., Witzani, L., Prayer, L., & Brugger, P. (2006). MRI of normal fetal brain development. *European Journal of Radiology*, 57: 199–216.

Prokosch, M., Yeo, R., & Miller, G. (2005). Intelligence tests with higher g-loadings show higher correlations with body symmetry: Evidence for a general fitness factor mediated by developmental stability. *Intelligence, 33:* 203-213.

Puma, M., Bell, S., Cook, R., Heid, C., Broene, P., Jenkins, F., Mashburn, A. & Downer, J. (2012). Third Grade Follow-Up to the Head Start Impact Study: Final Report. Office of Planning, Research and Evaluation Report 2012-45. *Administration for Children & Families*.

Quartz, S., & Sejnowski, T. (1997). The neural basis of cognitive development: A constructivist manifesto. *Behavioral and brain sciences, 20:* 537-556.

Reich, D. (2018). *Who we are and how we got here: Ancient DNA and the new science of the human past.* New York: Pantheon Books.

Renthal W. & Nestler, E. (2009). Chromatin regulation in drug addiction and depression. *Dialogues in Clinical Neuroscience,* 11:257-68.

Rietveld, C., Esko, T., Davies, G., Pers, T., Turley, P., Benyamin, B., Chabris, C., Emilsson, V., Rindermann, H., Becker, D., & Coyle, T. (2016). Survey of expert opinion on intelligence: Causes of international differences in cognitive ability tests. *Frontiers in psychology, 7:* 399.

Ritchie, S. (2015). *Intelligence: All that matters.* London: John Murray.

Robbins, B. & Ross, A. (1996). Response by Social Text editors Bruce Robbins and Andrew Ross. *Lingua Franca,* July/August.

Rogers, D., Deshpande, O., & Feldman, M. (2011). The spread of inequality. *PloS One, 6:* e24683.

Rose, S. (2009). Should scientists study race and IQ? No: Science and society do not benefit. *Nature, 457:* 786-788.

Rowe, D. (1994). *The limits of family influence: Genes, experience, and behavior.* Guilford Press.

Rowe, D., Jacobson, K., & Van den Oord, E. (1999). Genetic and environmental influences on vocabulary IQ: Parental education level as moderator. *Child development, 70:* 1151-1162.

Rundall, T., & Wheeler, R. (1979). The effect of income on use of preventive care: An evaluation of alternative explanations. *Journal of Health and Social Behavior,* 20: 397–406.

Rushton, J. (1990). Race and crime: A Reply to Roberts and Gabor. *Canadian Journal of Criminology, 32:* 315-334.

Sanger, R. (2015). IQ Intelligence Tests, Ethnic Adjustments and Atkins. *American University Law Review, 65:* 87-150.

Schlinger, H. (2003). The myth of intelligence. *Psychological Record, 53:* 15-32.

Schmidt, F. & Hunter, K. (2004). General mental ability in the world of work: Occupational attainment and job performance. *Journal of Personality and Social Psychology,* 86: 162-173.

Schön, R., & Silvén, M. (2007). Natural parenting—back to basics in infant care. *Evolutionary Psychology, 5: 102-183.*

Schultz, W., Kelli, H., Lisko, J., Varghese, T., Shen, J., Sandesara, P., Quyyumi, A., Taylor, H., Gulati, M., Harold, J. & Mieres, J. (2018). Socioeconomic status and cardiovascular outcomes: challenges and interventions. *Circulation, 137:* 2166-2178.

Schwartz, J., Savolainen, J., Aaltonen, M., Merikukka, M., Paananen, R., & Gissler, M. (2015). Intelligence and criminal behavior in a total birth cohort: An examination of functional form, dimensions of intelligence, and the nature of offending. *Intelligence, 51:* 109-118.

Schwekendick, D. (2009). Height and weight differences between North and South Korea. *Journal of Biosocial Science,* 41:446-454.

Seligman, D. (1992). *The question of intelligence: The IQ debate in America.* New York: Birch Lane Press.

Selita, F., & Kovas, Y. (2019). Genes and Gini: what inequality means for heritability. *Journal of iosocial Science, 51:* 18-47.

Sesardic, N. (2003). Heritability and indirect causation. *Philosophy of Science,* 70:1002-10014.

Shaw, P., Lerch, J., Greenstein, D., Sharp, W., Clasen, L., Evans, A., Giedd, J., Castellanos, F. & Rapoport, J. (2006). Longitudinal mapping of cortical thickness and clinical outcome in children and adolescents with attention-deficit/hyperactivity disorder. *Archives of General Psychiatry, 63:*540-549.

Shi, S., Cheng, T., Jan, L., & Jan, Y. (2004). The immunoglobulin family member dendrite arborization and synapse maturation 1 (Dasm1) controls excitatory synapse maturation. *Proceedings of the National Academy of Sciences, 101:* 13346-13351.

Shoda, Y., Mischel, W., & Peake, P. (1990). Predicting adolescent cognitive and self-regulatory competence from preschool delay of gratification: Identifying diagnostic conditions. *Developmental Psychology,* 26: 978–986.

Silver, I. (2019). Linear and non-linear: An exploration of the variation in the functional form of verbal IQ and antisocial behavior as adolescents age into adulthood. *Intelligence, 76,* 101375.

Simpson-Kent, I., Fuhrmann, D., Bathelt, J., Achterberg, J., Borgeest, G., & Kievit, R. (2020). Neurocognitive reorganization between crystallized intelligence, fluid intelligence and white matter microstructure in two age-heterogeneous developmental cohorts. *Developmental Cognitive Neuroscience, 41:* 100743.

Sjölund, S., Allebeck, P., & Hemmingsson, T. (2012). Intelligence quotient (IQ) in adolescence and later risk of alcohol-related hospital admissions and deaths—37-year follow-up of Swedish conscripts. *Addiction, 107:* 89-97.

Snyderman, M. & Rothman, S. (1988). *The IQ controversy, the media and public policy.* New Brunswick, NJ: Transaction.

Sokal, A. (1996). Transgressing the boundaries: Toward a transformative hermeneutics of quantum gravity. *Social Text,* 46/47: 217-252.

Sokal, A. & J. Bricmont (1998). *Fashionable nonsense: Postmodern intellectuals' abuse of Science.* New York: Picador.

Sowell, E., Thompson, P., Leonard, C., Welcome, S., Kan, E., & Toga, A. (2004). Longitudinal mapping of cortical thickness and brain growth in normal children. *Journal of Neuroscience, 24:* 8223-8231.

Spencer, S., Logel, C., & Davies, P. (2016). Stereotype threat. *Annual review of psychology, 67:* 415-437.

Spirtes, P., Glymour, C. & Scheines, R. (2000). Causation, prediction, and search. Cambridge, MA: MIT Press.

Sprecher, S., Brooks, J.., & Avogo, W. (2013). Self-esteem among young adults: Differences and similarities based on gender, race, and cohort (1990–2012). *Sex roles, 69:* 264-275.

Stams, G., Brugman, D., Deković, M., Van Rosmalen, L., Van Der Laan, P., & Gibbs, J. (2006). The moral judgment of juvenile delinquents: A meta-analysis. *Journal of abnormal child psychology, 34:* 692-708.

Steele, C., & Aronson, J. (1995). Stereotype threat and the intellectual test performance of African Americans. *Journal of Personality and Social Psychology*, 69: 797–811.

Steenland, K., Henley, J., & Thun, M. (2002). All-cause and cause-specific death rates by educational status for two million people in two American Cancer Society cohorts, 1959–1996. *American journal of epidemiology, 156:* 11-21.

Sternberg, R., Grigorenko, E., & Bundy, D. (2001). The predictive value of IQ. *Merrill-Palmer Quarterly (1982-):* 1-41.

Sundet, J., Barlaug, D., & Torjussen, T. (2004). The end of the Flynn effect? A study of secular trends in mean intelligence test scores of Norwegian conscripts during half a century. *Intelligence, 32:* 349-362.

Tanner, M. (2019). What's missing in the war on poverty? *The Cato Institute.*

Taylor, S. (1991). *Health psychology* (2nd ed.). New York: McGraw-Hill.

Teasdale, T., & Owen, D. (2008). Secular declines in cognitive test scores: A reversal of the Flynn Effect. *Intelligence, 36:* 121-126.

Tingberg, B., & Nilsson, D. (2020). Child neglect-still a neglected problem in the global world: A review. *Journal of Advanced Pediatrics and Child Health, 3:* 038-046.

Turkheimer, E. (2000). Three laws of behavior genetics and what they mean. *Current Directions in Psychological Science, 9:* 160-164.

Turkheimer, E., Haley, A., Waldron, M., d'Onofrio, B., & Gottesman, I. (2003). Socioeconomic status modifies heritability of IQ in young children. *Psychological science, 14:* 623-628.

Tuvblad, C., & Baker, L. (2011). Human aggression across the lifespan: genetic propensities and environmental moderators. *Advances in genetics, 75*: 171-214.

Twardosz, S., & Lutzker, J. (2010). Child maltreatment and the developing brain: A review of neuroscience perspectives. *Aggression and violent behavior, 15:* 59-68.

Van Den Heuvel, M., Stam, C., Kahn, R., & Pol, H. (2009). Efficiency of functional brain networks and intellectual performance. *Journal of Neuroscience, 29:* 7619-7624.

Vold, G., Bernard, T., & Snipes, J. (1998). *Theoretical criminology.* New York: Oxford University Press.

Walsh, A. (1998). Religion and hypertension: Testing alternative explanations among immigrants. *Behavioral Medicine*, 24: 122-130.

Walsh, A. (2003). Intelligence and antisocial behavior. In A. Walsh & L. Ellis (Eds.), *Biosocial criminology: Challenging environmentalism's supremacy*, pp. 105–124). Huntington, NY: Nova Science.

Walsh, A. (2009a). Crazy by design: A biosocial approach to the age-crime curve. In Walsh, A & Beaver, K. (eds) *Biosocial criminology: New directions in theory and research*, pp. 154-175. New York: Routledge.

Walsh, A. (2009b). *Biology and Criminology: The biosocial synthesis.* New York: Routledge.

Walsh, A. (2022). Political Ideology and Happiness. *Mankind Quarterly, 62:* 660-686.

Ward, D. & Tittle, C. (1994). IQ and delinquency: A test of two competing explanations. *Journal of Quantitative Criminology*, 10:189-212.

Walters, G. (2022). Mediating the low verbal intelligence–early adult offending relationship with pro-aggression attitudes. *Criminal Justice and Behavior, 49:* 513-529.

Wechsler, D. (1958). *The measurement and appraisal of adult intelligence.* Baltimore, MD: Williams & Wilkins.

Weinhold, B. (2006). Epigenetics: The science of change. *Environmental Health Perspectives*, 114:161-167.

Wells, B. (1980). *Personality and heredity.* London: Longman.

Wilkinson, R. (2002). *Unhealthy societies: the afflictions of inequality.* London: Routledge.

Williams, M., Parker, R., Baker, D., Parikh, N., Pitkin, K., Coates, W., & Nurss, J. (1995). Inadequate functional health literacy among patients at two public hospitals. *Journal of the American Medical Association, 274:* 1677-1682.

Wilson, J., & Herrnstein, R. (1985). *Crime and Human Nature.* New York: Simon & Schuster.

Woodley, M. (2012). A life history model of the Lynn–Flynn effect. *Personality and Individual Differences, 53:* 152-156.

Woollett, K., & Maguire, E. (2011). Acquiring "the Knowledge" of London's layout drives structural brain changes. *Current biology, 21:* 2109-2114.

Wraw, C., Deary, I.., Gale, C., & Der, G. (2015). Intelligence in youth and health at age 50. *Intelligence, 53:* 23-32.

Wright, J., Dietrich, K., Ris, M., Hornung, R., Wessel, S., & Lanphear, B. (2008). Association of prenatal and childhood blood lead concentrations with criminal arrests in early childhood. *PLoS Medicine*, 5: 732–740.

Wrulich, M., Brunner, M., Stadler, G., Schalke, D., Keller, U., & Martin, R. (2014). Forty years on: Childhood intelligence predicts health in middle adulthood. *Health Psychology*, 33: 292–296

Yang, F., Hu, T., Chen, S., Wang, K., Qu, Z., & Cui, H. (2022). Low intelligence predicts higher risks of coronary artery disease and myocardial infarction: Evidence from mendelian randomization study. *Frontiers in Genetics, 13.* 756901.

Yang, J., Bakshi, A., Zhu, Z., Hemani, G., Vinkhuyzen, A., Lee, S., Robinson, M., Perry, J., Nolte, I., van Vliet-Ostaptchouk, J., & Snieder, H. (2015). Genetic variance estimation with imputed variants finds negligible missing heritability for human height and body mass index. *Nature Genetics*, 47: 1114-1120.

York, E. (2021). Summary of the latest federal income tax data, 2021 update. *Tax Foundation.* https://taxfoundation.org/publications/latest-federal-income-tax-data/

Yu, T., Chou, W., Chow, J., Lin, C., Tung, L., & Chen, K. (2018). IQ discrepancy differentiates levels of fine motor skills and their relationship in children with autism spectrum disorders. *Neuropsychiatric Disease and Treatment, 14:* 597-605.

Yun, I., & Lee, J. (2013). IQ and delinquency: The differential detection hypothesis revisited. *Youth violence and juvenile justice, 11:* 196-211.

Zigerell, L. (2017). Potential publication bias in the stereotype threat literature: Comment on Nguyen and Ryan (2008). *Journal of Applied Psychology, 102:* 1159–1168.

Zillmer, E., Archer, R., & Castino, R. (1989). Rorschach records of Nazi war criminals: A reanalysis using current scoring and interpretation practices. *Journal of personality assessment, 53:* 85-99.

Index

www.ingramcontent.com/pod-product-compliance
Lightning Source LLC
Chambersburg PA
CBHW050537270326
41926CB00015B/3275